CALAMARI COOKBOOK

CALAMARI COOKBOOK

EXPLORING THE WORLD'S CUISINES WITH SQUID

By Joseph Schultz & Beth Regardz

ILLUSTRATED BY BETH REGARDZ

CELESTIALARTS

Berkeley, California

ACKNOWLEDGEMENTS

Special thanks to the following people for their assistance, support, and participation in this project:

ARTS RESOURCE CENTER
NANCY AUSTIN
FRANKLIN AVERY
LYNNE BASEHORE
TOM BREZSNY
FAST EDY

ROBERT HAAVIE
HANK LEACH
B. MODERN
JIM PETERSEN
BILL REYNOLDS
PAULA SCHMIDT
ELIZABETH SCHNEIDER
PAUL SCHRAUB
MARY SCHULTZ
PAULA WOLFERT

CELESTIAL ARTS
P.O. Box 7327
Berkeley, California 94707

Cover photo by Robert Haavie
Cover photo concept and design by Beth Regardz
Composition by QuadraType, San Francisco

Library of Congress Cataloging-in-Publication Data

Schultz, J. S. F. T. W. (Joseph S. F. T. W.), 1951–
  Calamari cookbook.

  Includes index.

  1. Cookery (Squid) I. Regardz, Beth, 1940–
II. Title.
TX748.S68S38 1987   641.6′94   87-10073
ISBN 0-89087-365-8

Manufactured in the United States of America
First Printing, 1987
1 2 3 4 5 — 91 90 89 88 87

This edition is dedicated to the staff of India Joze,
for making it all possible, and to the love of my life
for making it worthwhile.

Jsftw

Mine is dedicated to Hilary, Helen & Harold
and to all my squid loving pals.

Beth Regardz

CONTENTS

RECIPES

CALAMARI IN THE WORLD OF COOKING

Common throughout the world's oceans, mainstay of the diet of whales and dolphins, calamari have played little part in the written histories of cuisine. Mention of them has tended to emphasize their limited appeal, the difficulty and pitfalls in their cooking.

The meteoric rise of calamari advocacy in this country has changed this situation beyond recognition. Teuthology, the study of the squid, parades the adaptive wonders of the humble squid. Artists in diverse media unveil its felicitously formed sensuality. Poets ponder the resonances between our lives and the squids'. Fashion designers find daring new solutions to the problems of taste.

But most of all, calamari stand revealed as food for all seasonings, equally at home in the most elaborately fashioned *haute cuisine* as in the most casually and quickly thrown together snack. Calamari belong to the cooks of all ages and lands. Economical, very quick cooking, tolerant of being frozen and thawed better than much seafood, the flowers of its tentacles and the smooth tenderness of its bodies are the perfect vehicles for exploring the exotic culinary terrains of the world past and present.

Since the opening of India Joze restaurant in Santa Cruz in the early 1970's, we have paraded the delights of little-known cuisines and foodstuffs before a large and heterogeneous clientele. The phenomenal response to the First International Calamari Festival, held on September 8, 1980, in the restaurant and the Santa Cruz Art Center where we're located, vastly exceeded our expectations. This enthusiasm announced in unmistakable terms the dawn of an era of calamari consciousness. The Friends of the Calamari was formed immediately by a group of concerned citizens—artists, dancers, writers, actors, cooks, and promoters—to deal with the avalanche of interest in everything calamari-esque that the festival had triggered. This book is one tentacle of a vast and growing squid movement.

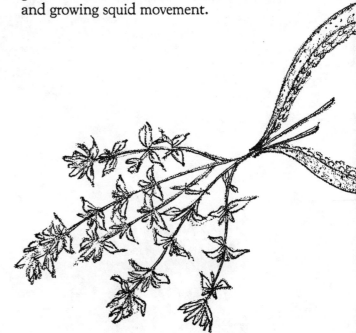

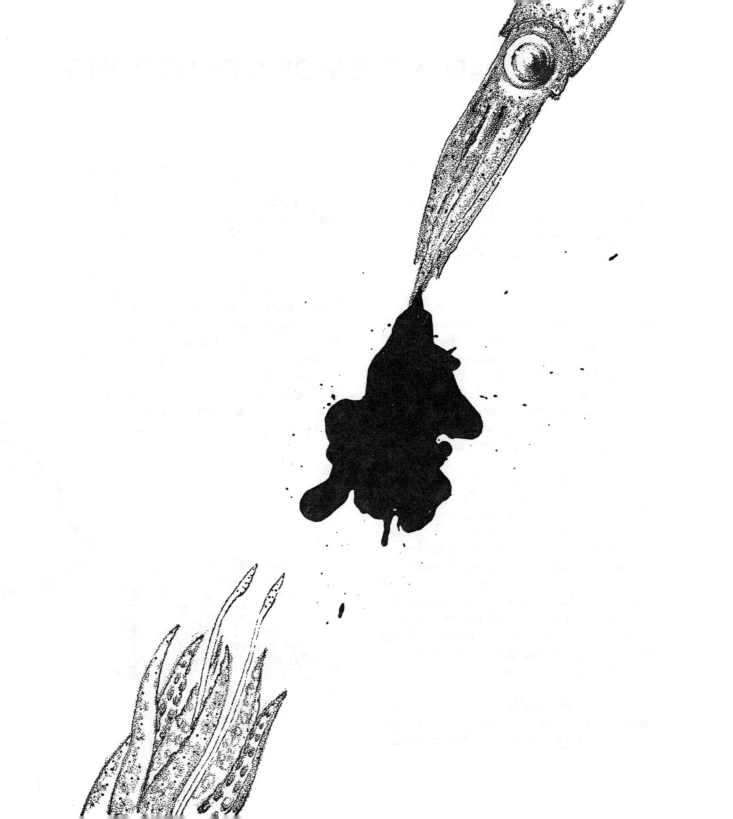

INTRODUCTION

Our intent in this book is twofold: to indicate how to cook with the humblest materials at hand in a way that is uplifting to the spirit and the body, and to suggest techniques whereby the most exotic and startling ingredients can enhance your repertoire of culinary maneuvers.

The squid is, we feel, uniquely suited to bridge these two modes of thought, being at once an inexpensive protein abundant beyond counting in all the world's oceans and the food most likely to provoke a shiver in the uninitiated.

The recipes in this collection have been selected as indicative of the varied cooking strategies used in locales frequented by squid. We offer these glimpses of a larger squid-eating reality in humility and reverence to the cooking spirits of all people. May these incomplete listings lead the reader to new explorations of delight and satisfaction.

The squid is very easy and quick to cook, though slightly messy to clean. The flavor is mild, and the texture, depending on the cooking technique, is tender-to-chewy-to-rubbery-to-crisp. Let us first address the manipulation of squid texture—texture being even more important than taste in this country. The edible portions are relatively homogeneous muscle tissue with little interstitial fat. So once the proteins are set and the liquids have come out of their delicate and succulent suspension, departing the tissues for the sauce, there is no backup of less easily lost juiciness.

In addition, too great a violence of cooking may prompt a rigor mortis-like reaction shrouding the delicacies of its taste in a most recalcitrant texture. There is less margin for error in cooking calamari than in cooking chicken, steak, or hamburger. It is all too easy to produce a dish that most people not used to squid will be unable to appreciate. We believe that it is mostly for this reason that many "tricks," "knacks," and "secrets" are always mentioned in connection with squid cuisine. We believe these should be seen as charms to ward off bad luck in cooking, not as hard-and-fast rules.

So when we cook calamari let us be fore-armed not only with knowledge and technique, but also with reverence and humility. Countless generations have evoked the meltingly tender promise of the squid in countless ways, ways that many times seem superficially contradictory. And many palates have tingled to dishes whose outcomes might well seem unsatisfactory to our tastes. We hope to offer strategies that will work with more than the few recipes herein contained.

First, let's look at the squid before we start cooking it. Raw *fresh* squid is like a stiff vibrant custard. *Fresh* squid. When it is frozen, unless it is frozen with a rapidity markedly unlikely, ice crystals form in the juices. As these grow, they pierce the cell walls, those walls which were keeping the squid vibrant. This is why the Japanese, who after all should know, insist on fresh fish for sushi.

But the issue is more complicated than this. Squid are captured during their mating season, which (as you may know) involves a shallow water orgy ending in egg-laying, then death (by exhaustion) of all parties. Let's face it, any squid caught after four solid days and nights of hard partying is going to be hard put to keep those cell walls up. Some cooks find that beating the meat is necessary to achieve relaxation of the tissue. It all depends when the squid were caught.

Frozen—thawed, which is almost the only way squid is *ever* sold, even in squid-inhabited regions, corresponds in texture to custard that has started to break down and become watery. Most of the recipes herein included involve modalities of the "medium-rare" texture: that point where the flesh is meltingly tender and juicy and the juices are just starting to flow into the sauce. Frozen—thawed squid *starts* at a "medium-rare" condition, hence cooking strategies need to be directed to keeping the cooking process from going too far, and driving all the juices out, which would be a strike against the quality of any dish made with such lean protein.

Most dishes call for adding squid very near the end of the cooking process, so it barely gets beyond heating up. Even so, the fluids in the squid start to emerge *fast*, just as over-cooked scrambled eggs get watery and grainy quickly. It is important to avoid the combination of thin, watery sauce and grainy, dry texture.

One strategy is to deep-fry the squid in a batter which absorbs or seals all the juices as they emerge. Deep-frying is probably the most popular form of squid consumption throughout the world. Many batters are possible; we have selected a Greek technique which best addresses the specific problems needing to be overcome in cooking squid, and is the easiest. The Chinese batter for sweet-and-sour squid is a different approach. While Japanese tempura is probably the most refined deep-frying technique, such wet batters are trickier to work with. The deep-frying method automatically adds the richness the calamari can use, and the browning of the batter is an easy visual cue to doneness. The only factor to watch is that the oil needs to be hot enough to crisp the batter before the squid gets too well done: tough, dry, rubbery. Alternatively, the squid can be shallow or deep-fried until it is totally crisp, as is done in Portugal. The succulence is then added in the form of an outside sauce, like mayonnaise, tartar sauce, or skordalia (see recipe, p. 120).

The wok approach cooks everything so fiercely and quickly that the juices are concentrated to a somewhat minimal glaze as they emerge from the pieces of squid. The outcome of a dish along these lines—Pad Mun Pla Phet, Tjumi-Tjumi Tjha, or Calamari Fra Diavolo, for example—is dependent on the amount of heat that can be brought to bear on the amount of food being cooked at one time. If the amount of food is large and the heat small (say, more than two servings at one time on a normal stove), the dish will water out faster than the liquid can be concentrated. In this case, the sauce will only be correctly intense long after the poor squid has been cooked to death. On the other hand, if the stove is hot and the amount of food small, small amounts of water may need to be sprinkled in during the cooking to keep the squid from drying, sticking, and burning as it cooks. The object of the cooking game in this sort of recipe is for the cooking to take place at precisely the right temperature. Obviously, the amount of liquid may need to be altered to achieve this, which changes the amount of other ingredients needed to reach a tasty balance.

There are further options in sautéeing a large amount of calamari. When the squid just starts to cook and release its juices, strain it out and concentrate the sauce down separately by heating and stirring to evaporate excess moisture. Or, if you want a lot of sauce, thicken the sauce with ground nuts, cornstarch, cheese, onions, flour, egg yolks, etc., as in recipes like Kalamarakia Me Saltsa, Squid with Lobster Sauce, Calamare en Mole Verde, and Calamares en su Tinta.

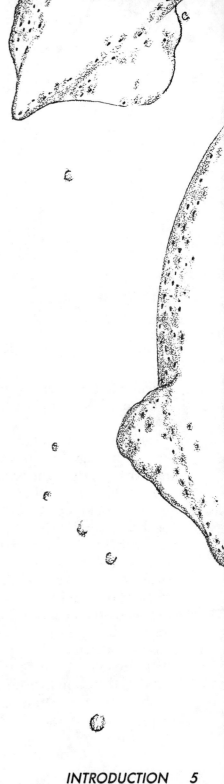

In these cases, get the sauce much drier or thicker than you actually want it, because it will thin out when you put the squid back in.

The total amount of heat used on a given amount of calamari tends to be more important than whether the cooking is fast or slow. A bare simmer in a sauce for several minutes could cook the squid *less* than two or three seconds in oil in a hot wok. The leeway in correct cooking duration varies from split seconds in a wok to minutes in a steamer. A lot of cold squid stirred into a small amount of hot sauce is going to cook differently than a little squid stirred into a lot of bubbling stew. The differences are difficult to quantify in a general way, as there are so many variables (stove heat, pan size and shape, and so on) even in a simple recipe. So rather than memorizing long lists of rules, think of the process from the squid's point of view.

Squid protein congeals in a manner similar to egg whites, but at a slightly higher temperature. The difference between high and low temperature cooking of squid is comparable to the difference between cooking scrambled eggs and cooking a custard, or a hard-boiled egg.

This may shed some light on why wok dishes call for thin rings or heavily cross hatched pieces to expose maximum surface area for quick heat penetration. On the other hand, a really long-simmered dish, such as Caldeirada, can get away with thick pieces because the heat penetration is so gentle that the outside doesn't overcook before the inside is ready.

Generally, we at India Joze cook squid only until it is just done, then serve it. There is another option. The constituents of squid which set up and become firm, then tough, are the same as the binding principles in other seafood, poultry, and meat. Long, gentle simmering in liquid does eventually dissolve those binders, leaving the squid, seafood, poultry, or meat somewhat stringy, but definitely tender and full of flavor from the sauce. This process can take anywhere from twenty minutes to an hour and a half with squid; there seems to be no way to tell in advance how long. Most of the sautéed dishes listed can be adapted to this method, which is also a way of saving an otherwise terminally over-toughened dish.

We have thus far focused primarily on considerations of texture in the final dish.

Americans are much more texture-conscious than other cultures; a strange taste is much more palatable to us than a weird texture. Slimy, stringy, grainy, rubbery on the negative side—meltingly tender, succulent, juicy on the positive side. These are the most common reactions to squid dishes.

So what about taste? In this realm we're in for a little good news and a little bad news. The good news is that squid has a very mild, unassertive flavor, capable of blending with the flavor of any sauce it is cooked in. The bad news is that squid has little quantity of flavor, unlike prawns or salmon, so the full responsibility for intensity and balance of flavor lies with the cook.

It is convenient for most culinary purposes to think of "taste" as an interplay between the five basic tastes—sweet, tart, salty, bitter, hot—and aromas, which are myriad and very difficult to classify. We have determined empirically that for a taste to be vivid and intense—which is not to say necessarily hot or spicy—some element of each of the five tastes needs to be present, and present in some sort of balance. Further, this presence and balance of flavors—which we call *flavor saturation*—is a necessary precondition to a full experience of the aroma or fragrance of a dish.

This point is difficult to demonstrate on paper. Consider the example of a soup tasting flat and boring until magically transformed by a little salt and lemon juice, revealing heretofore unsuspected subtleties

of flavor and aroma. Or perhaps a spicy tea whose spices are imperceptible until a little honey is added.

We have attempted in the following recipes to give some idea of the quantities of flavoring ingredients involved in the various dishes. It is only fair to say that we are doing so under protest, in full awareness that it may tend to draw a cook's attention away from how a dish tastes—which is the important thing—and towards how a recipe looks. There are no hard-and-fast rules for flavor saturation; some dishes are meant to be basically tart, like Dragon Squid, some dishes are meant to be hot and salty, like Pad Mun Pla Phet. One person's piquantly tart is another person's unbearably acrid, as one person's pleasantly tingly is another person's insufferably fiery. To complicate matters further, the same cook who created a dish which s/he finds a perfect taste counterpoint to a certain meal composed of certain dishes may find an exact duplicate of the dish brutally out of balance on a different occasion with different accompaniments.

All of our metabolisms change hour-to-hour and day-to-day and with them change our perceptions of sweet, tart, salty, bitter, and hot. Most ingredients in these recipes have more than one flavor; paprika, for example, both sweet and bitter, while lemon juice is tart with a varying amount of bitterness. Different batches have different characteristics, just as tomatoes vary greatly in their sweetness and tartness. Some, like onions and garlic, and many spices, vary their flavor balance according to the kind and amount of heat they are subjected to. Sometimes the elements are difficult to isolate and identify. For example, the sweetness in Adobo—a basically vinegary tart dish as usually cooked—comes from the pork itself and the tomato garnish, with some help from the massive amounts of garlic. The bitter comes from the black pepper and the garlic.

Suffice it to say that all of these recipes are designed to taste "good," and that most of the problems involved in dealing with new recipes—apart from problems of texture, which we toughed out earlier—can be solved by attention to the final flavor balance of a dish. If a dish is too tart, bring up the salty, bitter, hot, sweet levels. If it is too hot, increase the tart, bitter, salty, sweet levels. If it is too bland, bring up all the levels.

Luckily, the fragrances of a dish take care of themselves if the taste balance is right. Aromas don't conflict with each other. Of course, most aromatics have flavors as well. Ginger is hot and fragrant, while fresh mint is bitter and fragrant. The difficulty with substituting the dried versions of mint and ginger for the fresh is that the dried ones have more flavor than aroma, and may require more balancing than a delicate dish can take.

One last subject area, one which touches on many taboos. The reason "having a lot of fat in it" means "rich" in our language is probably because having a lot of fat in a dish enables one to get away with problems in the areas of texture, taste, and balance, just as being rich in the financial arena enables one to get away with problems in other arenas. The French for "fat," *matières graisses* sounds nicer, but then they don't need euphemisms, since they were never swayed by the controversies surrounding saturated fat and dietary cholesterol in the first place.

Fat is another dancer in flavor-balancing choreography. Certain flavors and aromas need a certain amount of fat present before they can be perceived. Fat can be emulsified and disguised so it doesn't seem like fat—mayonnaise, cheese, sour cream, and cold butter, for example. Or it can be blatant, unconcealed (and, hopefully, uncongealed) pools of richness—olive oil, ghee, peanut oil, lard—around and about a dish, as is found in the Indian, Middle Eastern, and Szechwan cuisines. Whatever form it takes, rich, heady, pungent flavors need more fat than clear, delicate ones. The Japanese appreciate the lean, delicate quintessence of squid itself. Hence they make up for this lost intensity with what is to us an extreme use of monosodium glutamate, or MSG.

We hope our introduction has not made the cooking of squid seem more tricky than it actually is. If you are unsure after all this about how a dish should taste, remember that you can always provide relishes or chutneys or sambals—hot ones, tart ones, slightly bitter ones, sweet-sour ones, salty

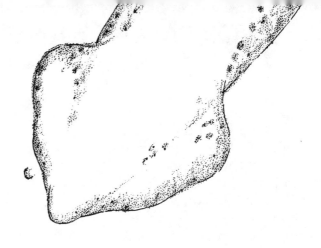

ones—so that the people can join you in the delights of taste combination and experimentation.

And, most importantly, we at India Joze will always be willing to advise and assist as far as we are able. You can reach us at the following address:

> 1001 Center St.
> Santa Cruz, California 95060
> (408) 427-3554

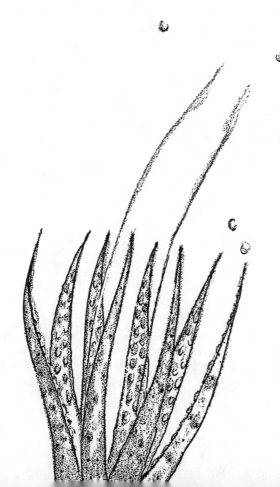

FLAVOR BALANCE AND SATURATION

The following listings are meant to illustrate the principles of flavor balancing, with reference to specific foods and flavorings. This list can be an aid in substituting certain ingredients for others, as well as a guide for generating new recipes from old. The listings are perforce incomplete and designed to be expanded upon.

An ingredient may be said to have a negative flavor, as potatoes are negatively salty, if its addition to a dish acts as if its presence diminishes the particular flavor element in a dish.

Good stocks and concentrated meat glazes act as flavor amplifiers in that they heighten perception of all the flavors. MSG amplifies flavors as well, but in a distorted way that may or may not be desirable. No attempt has been made to catalog the entries by relative intensity.

BITTER

black pepper (and hot)
tahini
chocolate and cocoa
tea
coffee
turmeric
artichokes
lemon, citrus peel
spinach
orange blossom water
scotch, bourbon
fried garlic, dark
green onions, raw (and hot)
fried onion, dark (not burned)
pomegranate (and tart)
asafoetida (fried in oil)
mustard seed (and sweet and hot,
    prepared mustard varies)
fried cinnamon (and sweet)
onion and garlic powder (too
    bitter, not recommended, though
    effective)
bell peppers, green
almond extract
capers
olives
cinnamon
cardamom
cloves (and sweet smelling)
rosewater
fried cumin
caviar (slightly)
coriander leaf
rue
watercress

SWEET

sugar
honey
molasses
cream
rum
fried garlic, light
fried onion, transparent, light
mirin—cooking sake
sherry
maple syrup
dried fruit
fruit (and tart)
miso (and salty)
paprika
bell peppers, red
white pepper (and hot)
tomatoes (some more than others)
caramel (less sweet than sugar,
    slightly bitter, can be not sweet
    at all)
mustard seed (and hot)

Negative Sweetness
heat

SOUR

lemon
tomato, raw, unheated·
tamarind
vinegars
grapefruit *(and bitter)*
lime *(and bitter)*
yogurt *(and related cultured milks)*
cheeses
omeboshi plums *(and salty)*
butter
sour cream
pomegranate
mango powder
wine
tart chutneys
pickles

OILY

oils
fats
butter *(and sweet, tart and salty)*
ghee *(butter oil)*
sour cream *(and tart)*
cream
cheese
nuts
peanut butter *(and salty)*
tahini *(and bitter)*
miso
caviar
sausage
bacon *(and sweet and salty)*
cream cheese
avocado

Negative Oiliness
emulsification of fats

SALTY

salt
butter
soy sauce
fish sauce
cheeses
anchovy paste
miso *(and sweet)*
olives
caviar
chutneys *(especially hot ones)*
Chinese black beans, salted
  preserved
hot bean sauce *(and variably hot,
  sour, bitter)*
pickles *(and tart)*
seaweeds *(some are saltier than
  others)*
preserved lemon *(and bitter)*
ham *(and sweet)*
bacon *(and rich and sweet)*
jerked beef

Negative Saltiness
potato

HOT

cayenne *(and bitter and sweet,
  when fried)*
chilis, fresh *(and bitter)*
black pepper *(and bitter)*
white pepper *(and sweet)*
horseradish *(and tart, when
  prepared)*
ginger, fresh *(and sweet)*
ginger, dried *(and bitter)*
garlic, raw, fresh
garlic powder *(and very bitter, not
  recommended generally)*
green onion, raw
hot chutneys
mustard seed *(less hot when fried)*
alcohol

Negative Hotness
parsley
coriander seed
cloves

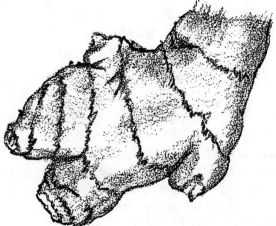

ADAPTATION OF NON-CALAMARI RECIPES TO CALAMARI AND VICE-VERSA

The squid is a mutable being, its close relative the cuttlefish even more so. Utilizing the closely packed chromatophores bespeckling their bodies, more properly called "mantles," these cephalopods can swim through an astonishing variety of colors and patterns.

As in life, so in the afterlife. The number of ways calamari has been cooked through the ages is only exceeded by the number of ways it could and shall be cooked in our enlightened calamari future. Producing successful dishes using calamari in lieu of other meats or vegetables requires only minor adjustments in cooking procedure in line with the special properties of calamari flesh.

First, consider the shape of the pieces being cooked. Although similar in taste to many other seafoods, any cut of squid is going to be thinner, and hence more quickly sensitive to the heat applied to it than scallops or abalone, for example. The cooking time used must be much shorter, and closely attended to. Now, some sauces used in cooking other foods acquire thickness, body, and a marriage of flavors during the time these other foods are cooked in them. But squid's cooking time is too brief to allow the sautéed onions in a dish like Kalamarakia Me Saltsa, for instance, to melt into succulence. Therefore, in adapting a recipe of this type, an extra step in which the sauce is simmered separately is necessary before the calamari is added. If the dish is baked slowly, as in many filet of sole dishes, the squid tends to relax into the sauce. However, the sauce of a baked squid dish may need to be carefully strained off and thickened by concentration or other means.

Second, calamari is very mild in flavor. This is scarcely a liability in a highly seasoned dish, but when calamari enters a dish designed for a food with a strong flavor of its own, beef or prawns for example, a little strategy is in order. Concentrated stocks are a useful means of retaining delicacy in a dish when replacing stronger-bodied foods, as stocks tend to bring all flavors more into a flavor saturated balance. If it seems appropriate, chicken, beef, pork, or lamb stocks concentrated down to a glaze can be added to calamari to enable it to stand in a recipe designed for any of those. Less time-consuming is the use of tiny dried shrimp, simmered and blenderized to make a sort of quick thick shrimp stock, that goes well in most recipes. Prepared oyster and fish sauces can help. And small amounts of meats, finely slivered to release lots of flavor into the sauce, are time-honored additions in the Chinese and Southeast Asian cuisines.

The various instant bouillons and all-purpose seasonings rely on hydrolized protein to give an effect similar to—we think inferior to—that produced by honest stocks.

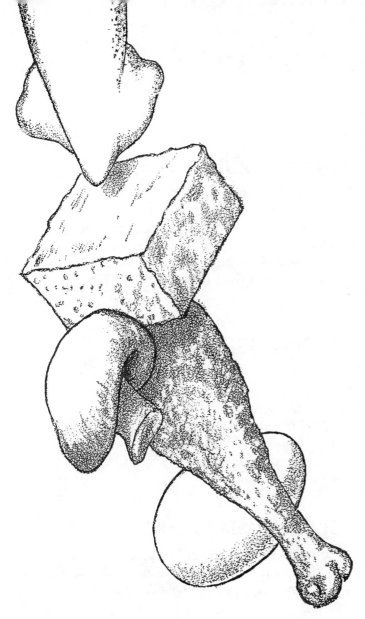

Like most seafood preparations adapted from other meat recipes, calamari requires extra richness in the final dish. Otherwise, the dish will tend to taste somewhat thin. This richness can come from extra oil used in cooking, or can be obtained more subtly by extra nuts blended into the sauce, or extra egg yolks, cream, sour cream, cheese, peanut butter, tahini, or cashew butter, depending on the individual recipe.

Some vegetarians feel that calamari are basically unusually mobile sea-going vegetables. Others prefer to exercise their calamari consciousness with less sentient raw materials. As squid has definite affinities with tofu and mushrooms, translation of recipes is simple. The challenges one encounters during the transformation of calamari to universally acceptable gastronomy are similar to those faced by vegetarians everywhere. Mushrooms, especially oyster mushrooms, chanterelles, and other exotic fungi, need only a brief sauté in some tasty fat to become rich and concentrated enough to substitute for calamari. Very fresh tofu can be treated precisely as squid in most recipes, though more delicately. Slightly older tofu or tempeh (a soy-mushroom loaf originally from Indonesia) profit from a more thorough browning in lots of fat before use.

This shortcut is so widespread that few speak against it. It leads to a pervasive sameness of flavors and a devaluing of culinary exploration. We see it as not in the true spirit of calamari cookery. Attention to flavor balance and intensity makes these shortcuts unnecessary.

Light meats, such as veal, sweetbreads, brains, chicken, and seafood, are even easier to adapt to squid recipes. Simply cut them into squid-sized pieces and treat as calamari.

BASIC RECIPES AND INGREDIENTS

The purpose of this section is to introduce you to some familiar and unfamiliar ingredients used in the recipes in this book. We have included the recipes for some basics like stock, as well as suggestions for using the various seasonings. (After some remarks on the squid itself, entries follow alphabetical order.)

The following notes and listings are perforce incomplete. A record of all the many helpful and delightful bits and routines we have found in all the world's cookings is far outside our scope. However, at the very least, these entries will guide you in making any necessary substitutions and in achieving flavor balance.

SQUID

Ten-armed cephalopods ranging in size from less than half an inch to a hundred feet long or more. The most commonly used species in this country are *Loligo opalescens* (West Coast) and *Loligo pealei* (East Coast). Japan is still the largest producer and consumer of squid, mostly *Ommastrephes sloanei* and *Ommastrephes vulgaris*. All varieties of squid cook similarly. The West Coast season is about June to November. They are commonly available frozen.

DRIED SQUID

In many parts of the world, squid is sold flattened, salted, and dried. Soak in warm water for forty-five minutes, clean as fresh frozen squid. Dried squid can be used in any recipe, allowing more cooking time. The texture of the finished dish will be more chewy.

CUTTLEFISH

A ten-armed cephalopod, *Sepia officinalis sp.*, closely related to and resembling squid. Heavier bodied, with a thick calcareous cuttlebone rather than a transparent flexible quill. More ink (our word "sepia" refers to this animal), and thicker fleshed. Cook as squid after cleaning.

BLACK MUSTARD SEED

Common flavoring in Indian cooking, fried in oil until it pops before use. Yellow mustard seed is not as sweet, but may be substituted.

CAROENUM

Wine concentrated down to half its original volume. An ancient Roman technique for intensifying wine flavor; especially appropriate to calamari cookery, as it lessens the need to concentrate sauces separately.

CHILI WATER

Rather than burn our eyes and fingertips mincing fresh hot chilis, we cut off the stems and blenderize them with a little water. The resulting paste is uniform in heat and wonderfully fresh tasting. We prefer fresh chili water to cayenne for making dishes hot because chili water does not require cooking or frying to develop its best flavor, and is thus easier to add little by little to obtain the desired level of hotness in a dish. Different varieties of chilis and different crops of the same variety vary greatly in heat, and other flavors. Always taste your chili water, cautiously, before adding it. Fresh chilis are often quite bitter as well as hot. Red chilis are riper and tend to be sweeter, though not necessarily less hot. They are also generally less available. If the flavor balance of your dish requires hotness and sweetness, cayenne soaked in vinegar for an hour or so may be a better choice than an exceptionally bitter batch of chili water. Fresh or canned pimentos or red bell peppers have the chili flavor without the hotness, if such is desired.

COCONUT MILK

See under Stocks.

CURRY LEAF

Not curry powder and nothing like it. An aromatic leaf fried lightly before use in Indian cooking. Very similar to the *daun salaam* leaf used in Indonesian cooking and interchangeable with it.

DRIED SHRIMP

Used as an ingredient in Latin American, African, and Oriental cuisine. Available in many supermarkets. They are soaked, then ground up or used whole.

FERMENTED BEANS (AND GRAINS)

All the fermented bean products used throughout the Far East have similar abilities to give body and duration of flavor to foods. They are used analogously to fermented fish products in Southeast Asia. Judicious substitution among and between these two groups of flavorings can be successful. All keep indefinitely, covered and refrigerated.

MISO   Various Japanese fermented bean and grain pastes, all salty. Some types are sweeter, more chunky, tarter, saltier, more winey than others. The dark types tend to be a little heavy for use with calamari.

BEAN SAUCES   Yellow, brown, red, black, soy, hot, chili, broad, Szechwan—usually Chinese. Some versions of these are heavily sweetened for use in pastries, outside of which they have limited utility. Check the labels carefully. All are quite strong in flavor, and different from each other, though used in similar ways.

HOT BEAN SAUCE OR PASTE
Available ready-made. If you fail to find a brand you particularly like, you can

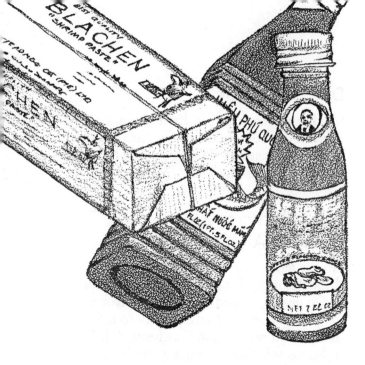

experiment making your own from miso or Chinese bean sauce. In this way, you can get exactly the balance you desire.

HOT BEAN PASTE
peanut oil
cayenne
fresh ginger, paste or slivers
garlic paste (*see garlic paste recipe*)
sugar or brown sugar, molasses, or
    honey
miso, or any type of fermented or
    Chinese bean sauce will make a
    good sauce
sherry or white wine
rice wine vinegar

That's right, no amounts for this recipe, just technique. All the permutations of this preparation are useful; fuss with it until it tastes right. Basi-

cally, fry the cayenne, ginger, and garlic any amount short of burning. Lightly fry the sugar to caramelize (not necessary with honey). Stir in wine, then miso. After a short simmer, it is often useful for the sauce to be as thick as honey or a light cream sauce. Balance the taste with rice wine vinegar, and then with more of any of the ingredients that seem lacking.

FERMENTED FISH PRODUCTS

Some of the strangest flavors to deal with for most Westerners are the fishy flavorings. Quite common in the luxurious cooking of ancient Rome, the tantalizingly sensual undercurrents these provide have faded from modern usage to token tubes of anchovy paste. It can be difficult to convince a cook that something with an objectionable reek can have an important place in his/her cuisine. But it is part of calamari's culinary mission to help us all appreciate the scorned, the lowly ingredients.

SHRIMP PASTE   Known as *trassi* or *blachan* in Indonesia, *kapi* in Thailand, this hard-to-crumbly block is always fried in oil or roasted before use. The frying/roasting process generates some powerful fumes. *Black shrimp paste* is known in Indonesia as *petis*. This sticky, dark paste is mostly used in salads and cold dishes. In emergencies, it does give somewhat the same flavor. It is not fried the way trassi is.

FISH SAUCE   Also known as *nam pla*, fish's gravy. Fermented, brined fish extract imported from Southeast Asia or China. Available as a clear brown liquid—Thai, Viet, Chinese style—or as a thin murky pink paste—Bagoong, Philippine style. Very fishy, very, very salty. Similar to the ancient Roman flavoring "liquamen." Used discreetly, the flavor is an important background element. Substitute anchovy paste or anchovy filet mashed in water. Soy sauce can be used, but lacks the requisite body. Miso is a closer substitute.

OYSTER SAUCE   Opaque brown salty extract of partially fermented oysters. Used in Chinese and Indonesian dishes. Can replace fermented fish or shrimp products if those are objectionable or unattainable. Keeps indefinitely.

GARLIC PASTE

Remove outer skin, roots, and heavy center stem from 2 or 3 bulbs of garlic. It is not necessary to skin the individual cloves. Place cloves in blender with water to cover. Blend at highest speed until a smooth paste is formed. For maximum smoothness, the mixture should be thick enough to just barely blend. Too thin and the skins don't get pulverized. Too thick and nothing blends. Adjust consistency with more water or garlic if necessary. The finished paste may be strained if fibers remain. Kept tightly covered in the refrigerator, it maintains a superlative freshness for at least 4 days. Most cooks are unable to detect a deterioration in quality for at least a week. Other forms of fresh garlic may substitute, but not store-bought garlic paste or dried garlic products.

GHEE

See under Oils.

GINGER

Common in the tropical cuisines, fresh ginger is an aromatic that can be added at different parts of the cooking process for different effects. Select firm, fresh rhizomes. Dried ginger has different and more limited uses. Do not carelessly substitute one for the other.

HERBS

Fresh herbs are usually quite different from their dried counterparts: much stronger in fragrance and milder in flavor, much more likely to augment a dish than throw off the flavor balance. The Viets, Thais, and Indonesians use many fresh herbs unavailable in this country. A better sense of the light aromatic-ness of their flavors is gained by using fresh aromatics, even non-traditional ones, than by opening old dried-out packets of herbs.

FRESH CORIANDER LEAF Also known as cilantro. Crucial to a large number of the world's cuisines. The leaves resemble flat-leaf parsley, with a penetrating flavor that is totally without substitute. We especially discourage the use of dried coriander leaves. Some people have an aversion to the flavor, based in part in experience of the overuse of less-than-perfectly fresh or dried leaves in certain dishes. It is an important background flavor in calamari cookery because of its ability to heighten other flavors, especially spicy ones. People who like it are often passionate about it. It is increasingly available in Mexican and Chinese markets. It is also very easy to grow from seed, even from the whole seeds sold as spices.

FRESH MINT A delicate and unobtrusive flavor, with a delightful aroma, fresh mint can be a part of many of the dishes in many cuisines. Dried mint has much more limited utility.

FRESH TARRAGON, FRESH CHERVIL, FRESH PARSLEY, FRESH CHIVES, FRESH DILL Often used in dried form, all of these basically European herbs lose essential parts of their charm when dried. Better to use what fresh herbs you do have than substitute dried.

FRESH BASIL, FRESH OREGANO, FRESH MARJORAM, FRESH SAVORY, FRESH THYME, FRESH ROSEMARY, FRESH BAY These herbs all have interesting uses in both their fresh and dried forms. The fresh and dried forms are not equivalents; the fresh tend to be thinner, sharper, brighter, and more heady and the dried more mellow, more blending in the background, more thick. Calamari is adept at going both ways, so decide what effects you want.

KATSUOBUSHI

Japanese dried bonito flakes. Used with *kombu* (kelp) to make the important Japanese cooking stock. Use about 1/2 cup bonito flakes and a 3-inch square of kelp to a quart of water. Simmer 2–3 minutes, strain well. Keeps at room temperature about 8 hours, refrigerated about 2 days.

KENTJUR

Similar to and interchangeable in use with *laos*.

LAOS

An aromatic spice in the ginger family; much used in Indonesia. Gives a heady, distinctive flavor if not used to excess.

MANGO POWDER

Dried ground mango imported from India. Used to make dishes tart. Rhubarb chopped and simmered in a little water gives somewhat the same tart astringency.

MAYONNAISE

1 egg
1/8–1 tsp. dry mustard *or* 1/4–1 tsp. if prepared French or German style mustard
1/2 tsp. salt, to taste
1/2–1 tsp. garlic paste
1–2 Tbs. lemon juice or wine vinegar
1–4 tsp. chopped fresh herbs: any combination of parsley, tarragon, oregano, dill, scallions, chives, sweet basil, thyme
dash freshly ground pepper
3/4–1 cup good oil, preferably olive oil

This is harder to explain than to do, especially when done in a good blender capable of blending small amounts efficiently. Blend egg alone at medium speed for about 15 seconds. Add mustard and blend 5–10 seconds longer. Add salt, garlic, lemon juice, herbs, pepper. With the blender running on "high," slowly pour in the oil. At this point, the sauce should start to thicken heavily. Keep adding oil until the mixture is too thick to blend. This will probably take about 2/3 to 3/4 cup oil. Stop blender, check and adjust taste balance. If it is too sticky and not creamy enough at this point, blend in a couple tablespoons of boiling water, then add more oil.

Numerous other methods exist, all of which can be adapted to these ingredients. At the simplest, some of the flavorings of this recipe could be folded into commercial mayonnaise.

MUSTARD SEED

See under Black mustard seed.

NATURAL FOODS

Brown rice, honey, whole wheat flour, and so on. Western civilization's latest acts of imperialism are on the culinary front. When not borrowing other cultures' techniques and calling them our own—"La Nouvelle Cuisine"—we presume to tell them how they could improve their cooking. Squid-fried rice (Nasi Goreng) can be made with brown rice, Sweet-and-Sour Squid can be made with honey, but is our culture and science so unquestionably superior that we should be dictating changes in someone else's? Follow your own aesthetic.

OILS

All cooking oils are somewhat interchangeable, that is, they will work for each other. The authentic and unique qualities of many dishes are strongly affected by the oils used, but any oils used should taste good to you. It is difficult to disguise the flavor of an oil you consider crummy for any reason. Following are a few of our favorites.

PEANUT OIL   Stable at high temperatures, best for woking.

OLIVE OIL   Important flavor for Mediterranean area dishes.

SESAME OIL, ROASTED   Flavoring oil, not cooking medium. Added to Chinese dishes after cooking.

SESAME OIL, LIGHT   Cooking oil in Burma and parts of India. Mild flavor can be approximated by a couple of drops of roasted sesame oil in other oils.

CLARIFIED BUTTER & GHEE   Indian butter oil. Make ghee by melting butter over medium heat and simmering until the solids brown lightly, then straining off the clear liquid. A nuttier flavor than clarified butter, which is made by melting butter and straining the oil off before the solids toast. Both are useful and stable at very high temperatures. Some Indians even recommend making ghee from rancid butter to heighten the buttery flavor.

BUTTER   Will burn at high temperatures, but correctly used, butter adds tartness and body as well as richness to dishes. Oils substitute better for clarified butter than for butter because butter is more than just oil.

DENDÊ OIL   Brazilian or African unrefined palm oil. Orange color, penetrating flavor. Always added at the end of cooking processes, the way roasted sesame oil is used in China, but in greater quantities. Other oils simmered with paprika or annatto (achiote) seeds and strained will give much the same color. Annattoized oil has a similar amount of flavor, though a different one.

ORIENTAL VEGETABLES

Increasingly common in supermarkets are Chinese (Napa) cabbage and bok choy. They are mild flavored and easy to use. Daikon, giant white radish, bean sprouts, and snow peas are commonplace. If you wish to experiment with the more exotic ones, remember that they are usually cooked lightly. Some are supposed to be very bitter, so take that into account with your flavor balancing.

SHRIMP, DRIED

See under Dried shrimp.

STOCKS AND COCONUT MILK

Many recipes call for the use of stocks or water. Stocks' amazing abilities to heighten all flavor have seemingly fallen into disuse with the decline in the importance of soups and the rise of the use of canned and instant bouillons containing hydrolized protein. Organized and dedicated cooks will never let true stocks entirely disappear. Pressure cookers and fine chopping of the ingredients can speed up the process of making stocks. All stocks profit from concentration. They can be very much more or less elaborately constructed; but even a hurried stock is better than none at all. They keep under refrigeration for three to four days and can be frozen indefinitely.

BROWN STOCK
In a hot oven, roast beef and/or veal bones, scraps, and trimmings until light brown (most conveniently in the pan you will simmer them in), along with an onion and/or onion skins. Add salt, other vegetables (especially carrots and celery), maybe some parsley, garlic, and a couple of other herbs, but not too many. Cover with water and bring to a boil; simmer for a couple of hours or pressure cook; strain, skim off excess fat (some is fine).

CHICKEN OR PORK STOCK
Use necks, backs, scraps, gizzards, bones. Cover with water, add some vegetables and herbs and garlic, bring to a boil; simmer for a couple hours or pressure cook; strain, skim off excess fat.

SEAFOOD STOCK
See also Katsuobushi. Use fish heads, bones, shrimp shells, trimmings. Add some wine, a little wine vinegar, carrots, onions, celery, parsley, salt, peppercorns, herbs as desired. Simmer everything half an hour or so. Strain.

VEGETABLE STOCK
A good, strong, balanced vegetable stock is more difficult to achieve than meat, poultry, or seafood stocks. A combination of onion, celery, carrot, and a little cabbage with parsley, garlic, and bay leaf makes a good stock, if lightly browned first in good fat and then well simmered and concentrated. Any bean soaking or cooking water is very useful to give body. Water used to soak Asian shiitake mushrooms also gives wonderful flavor.

COCONUT MILK
Not exactly a stock, but used very similarly in the tropics. Crack a coconut and pry out the meat. Blend the meat, the liquid inside, and 3 cups very hot water in a blender or food processor until smooth. Strain in a fine sieve or colander lined with cheesecloth, pressing as hard as possible on the pulp to extract the flavor and oil. Let stand in the refrigerator an hour or so. The milk at the top is the thick milk. We do not recommend the use of dried coconut. A tastier substitute would be water with sour cream blended in just before the squid is cooked to give equivalent body. Coconut milk is highly perish-

able. Keeps about one day, well refrigerated. Freeze for longer storage.

TAMARIND

Available as whole dried pods in Latin American markets. Available as partially seeded blocks and concentrate in Asian markets. The tart fruit of a tropical tree. The dried pod is soaked in boiling water, lightly blenderized. The pulp is sieved or food-milled to remove the seeds and fibers. Provides a mild thick tartness that doesn't change with simmering. Lemon juice or vinegar can substitute for the tartness. Blenderized dried apricots and water can provoke reminiscences of its fleshiness. The pods keep indefinitely. The soaked pulp keeps about four days under refrigeration.

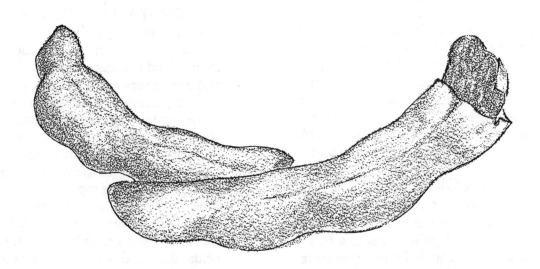

SOURCES FOR EXOTIC INGREDIENTS

We have tried to indicate in our introductory remarks that no ingredient is indispensable, that attention to and understanding of the role a given ingredient plays in a given dish makes it possible to select available substitutes both sincere and appropriate, if not authentic.

After all, "authenticity" has always been developed by cooks alert to the possibilities of change within the givens of a particular culture.

It is still diverting and stimulating to the culinary imagination to use materials from outside the context of one's culture, just as through travel and the unfamiliar, one finally begins to truly appreciate home and the familiar.

The following stores will accept mail orders.

Haig's Delicacies
642 Clement St.
San Francisco, Cal. 94118
(415) 752-6283
> Full line of Middle Eastern, Indian, and Far Eastern spices, condiments, and preserved foods.

Ratto's
821 Washington St.
Oakland, Cal. 94607
(415) 832-6503
> Large variety of specialty cooking paraphernalia, spices, and preserved foods.

Bezjian's Grocery, Inc.
Attn: Jack Bezjian
4725 Santa Monica Blvd.
Los Angeles, Cal. 90029
(213) 663-1503
> International delicacies.

Oriental Import–Export Co.
2009 Polk St.
Houston, Texas 77002
(713) 223-5621
> Chinese ingredients.

Vietnam House
191 Farmington Ave.
Hartford, Conn. 06105
(203) 524-0010
> Southeast Asian ingredients.

BATTERIE DE CUISINE: EQUIPMENT, IMPLEMENTS, HARDWARE

The possibilities for culinary journeying through calamari cookery span the history of food. No one slant on food preparation, no single cook's sense of the rightness of foods, is sufficient to pursue the avenues and byways, the directions and indirections of gastronomic exploration.

Hence, no exhaustive inventory of the tools and toys of cooking is possible. New and amusing techniques will continue to spring up as long as there are people delighting in cooking. We maintain that the object of a gadget should be to make any important process easy and fun enough to be worth doing. Two of the signs of good cooks are that they perceive many distinctions as crucial to the success of a dish or a meal—be these elements of presentation, niceties of flavoring, precisely desired consistencies, or ideological purity of ingredients—and that they are efficient and fast enough in the steps of cooking—shopping, chopping, food-on-the-plate-plopping, around-the-kitchen-hopping—to avoid becoming frustrated by an inability to do the things they think should be done in the time they want to spend cooking. For example, some cooks who appreciate the succulence of finely diced sautéed onions in a dish are unwilling to spend the time these take unless they have the aid of a food processor. For these cooks, a food processor is a logical tool. For someone whose boredom threshold for chopping by hand is higher, for whom knife work is a meditation, a food processor is a frill. Our personal preference is for simple, high quality tools capable of performing the necessary operations easily.

KNIFE

Squid are difficult to hack with a dull knife. Depending how dull the knife is, anything from rubbing it lightly on a sharpening steel or the bottom of a china plate, to a heavier rubbing (whetting) on a sharpening stone or a smooth sidewalk, to a total reshaping of the blade's edge on a grindstone (preferably by a professional) may be necessary to restore the ease and pleasure of a sharp knife. And there are innumerable knife sharpening gadgets on the market, many of which are not too injurious to a knife's long life.

Any type knife that's comfortable for you to use is fine. We have found that the precise and minute chopping of the ingredients found in the Asian recipes is best accomplished with a thin, Chinese pattern slicing–cleaver. The initial awkwardness of dealing with such a large blade is soon overcome, and the handiness of having a wide blade for carrying little bits of flavoring materials from the cutting board to the pan is worth the trouble. A cleaver *must* be kept sharp or its clumsiness is intensified.

Squid tends to bring a rusty flavor out of a carbon steel blade even more quickly than fruit, so we recommend whatever knife used be stainless steel. Mastery of one sharp knife tends to be more effective than possession of many dull ones.

BLENDER

Unpacking the flavor of many foods involves breaking down the cell structures to release the juices, volatile oils, fats, and so on, trapped within. Thinly sliced *fresh* vegetables taste so much more vivid than coarsely chopped ones because (for those of us who do not chew each bite thoroughly, thoroughly, thoroughly) more flavor is available in the mouth and on the tongue before the bite is swallowed. On the other hand, thinly sliced ingredients have more surface area exposed to the air, and hence their flavors degrade and are lost more rapidly, if they are not prepared immediately prior to serving.

The tool of choice to perform what we use a blender to approximate is the large mortar and pestle. Nuts, seeds, spices, and coconut are all examples of highly concentrated foods requiring extreme pulverization to attain the fullness of flavor and satiny smoothness which give body, richness, and savor to dishes rather than scratchiness, roughness, and stick-to-the-roof-of-the-mouthness.

Unfortunately, appropriately large and smooth mortar and pestle sets are difficult to obtain and even more difficult to learn to use efficiently or neatly. So the high-pitched scream of a blender pushed to its limits is a common adjunct to an adventurous kitchen. For a blender to grind substances like sesame seeds, coconut, or in-the-skin garlic with anything like the requisite thoroughness, the motor must be powerful, high-speed, and capable of sustained operation for several minutes at a time. A wide selection of speeds is irrelevant to most purposes, although our features-not-performance oriented manufacturers tend to put the largest motors in the most gimmicky housings.

Any blender, including the often adequate junk store models, will only grind mixtures completely if they are of a consistency just barely thin enough to blend. Too thin, and the hard pieces whirl around without getting chopped. Too thick, and the partially blended mass solidifies above the blades of the blender without blending at all. Small amounts of the liquid or solids need to be added during the blending process to maintain this ideal consistency.

A blender with a jar of small diameter at the bottom near the blades, an Osterizer, is the best for blending the small quantities often needed.

Important note: If blending a hot liquid—for example, blending nuts into a cooking sauce to thicken it—be extremely careful. The pressure which builds up the instant you turn the blender on will blow the lid off and scald you. The harder you hold the lid on, the worse the explosion. For your safety, cover the mouth of the jar with a cloth before turning it on so the pressure can whoosh out harmlessly without the contents of the blender following suit.

On the last problem with blenders: the noise can be excruciating. It may be worth your time arranging a cupboard or closet with a tight-fitting door so you can shut the blender in while it is blending.

WOK AND SPATULA

This pan was developed in those parts of the world concerned with precise nuances of flavoring through heat treatment, with efficient use of limited fuel, with safe and economical deep-frying, and with maximization of flavor through concentration of cooking bases.

The cornerless, hemispherical shape matches the curve of the spatula to afford maximum control of small quantities of spices being fried, while at the same time facilitating the admixture of larger quantities of last-second additions to various dishes.

Woks are designed for fast, high-intensity cooking, by and large. Most home stoves are not hot enough to make the best use of a wok, although the flame height on gas stoves is easily adjusted to partially rectify this deficiency. Electric stoves and electric woks . . . let us pass to a pleasanter subject . . . No, seriously, cooking on an electric stove on the maximum setting is much like cooking over charcoal, which is, after all, what woks were designed for. Proper prior planning prevents pitifully poor performance: a readiness to snatch the wok from the heat and/or add water in amounts calculated to regulate the heat without sogging-out what is being cooked makes possible a reasonable level of control and flexibility.

Flat-bottomed woks have limited utility, as they lack the thickness which enables a cast-iron skillet to store heat and maintain high frying temperatures, as well as lacking other benefits associated with a wok's shape. The stability lacking in a conventional wok on a conventional stove is better gained by somehow affixing a ring stand to one burner of your stove. The usefulness of a wok setup which does not need to be steadied with one hand while you stir with the other is hard to overemphasize.

This stability is especially important when deep-frying. The shape of a wok is such that two cups of oil is deep enough for most deep-frying purposes. The wide rim prevents the oil from boiling over and out and gives room for a rack to let the finished fritters drain.

Choose a large wok; the more surface area, the faster sauces can be concentrated down. Most woks, and all the inexpensive ones, are spun from steel and are not designed to have acid food in them for any length of time. Tomatoes, lemon juice, tamarind, vinegar, fruits, and so forth, should be added only at the very end of cooking, or a metallic taste in the final dish is the result. Stainless steel woks are only a partial answer; the heat transfer is so uneven by comparison with steel, especially at high temperatures, that a large copper-clad stainless or enameled cast-iron or Caphalon (anodized aluminum) skillet is preferable, until we come out with the ultimate wok.

POTATO RICER

If you use a lot of coconut milk, you will save time and get more milk out of your coconuts if you have a tool to squeeze the pulp with immense pressure. A colander lined with cheesecloth and pressed with a plate or bowl is an acceptable, if tedious, substitute.

SPICE GRINDER

Once you have used freshly ground aromatics it is difficult to return to the pallidness of old, pre-ground spices. Turmeric, fenugreek, and dried ginger are difficult to grind without breaking your grinder, and besides, they are little used as aromatics, more as background spices. But cardamom, cinnamon, cloves, fennel, cumin, black and white pepper, and many others are revelations in a freshly ground state. Spices must be ground thoroughly, or the husks and pieces of chaff give an unpleasant roughness to dishes. Sift them out if necessary.

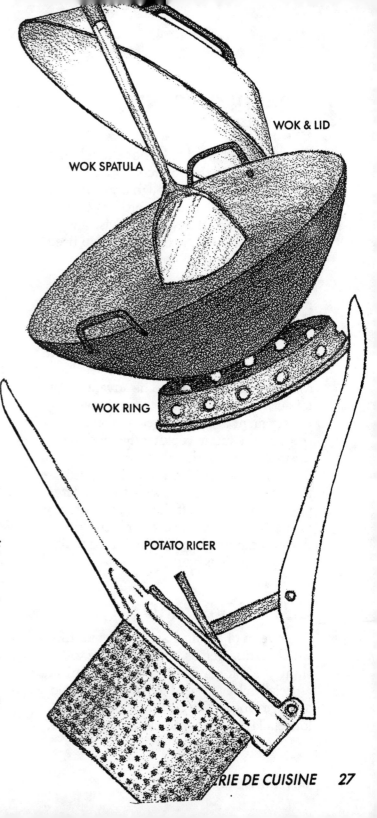

WOK & LID

WOK SPATULA

WOK RING

POTATO RICER

HIBACHI OR OTHER BRAZIER

Broiling setups need to be hot enough to sear food before they overcook it. If your oven broiler isn't hot enough even when it is long preheated, consider broiling over charcoal. You might even improvise a way to set your wok over charcoal when you need more heat than your stove puts out.

ORIENTAL STEAMERS

Oriental steamers look like bamboo mesh baskets nestling inside each other. They are used in a wok with some water in the bottom for gentle steaming. The advantage of an authentic steamer over an improvised arrangement is that the steam percolates through the mesh, cooking the food then dissipating out, rather than condensing and falling back on the food to thin the delicate flavors. Use a plate that will fit into a large pot and hold it up off the bottom with a rack or a bowl for an acceptable substitute. A towel can be placed under the lid to absorb the condensation.

CUTTING BOARD

After years of building and using beautiful wood cutting boards, we are coming to think the soft plastic ones superior. Knives, especially cleavers used for chopping, hold an edge longer. The cutting boards last longer. They are easy to clean and sterilize.

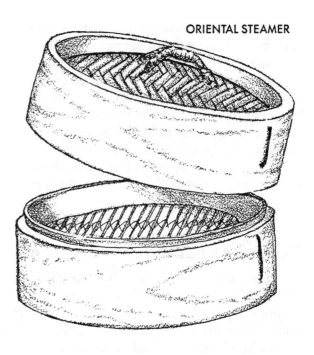

ORIENTAL STEAMER

Both hard and soft types exist. The soft ones are often white, polypropylene, and less expensive. When using any lightweight cutting board for chopping, cushion it with a towel on a solid surface. Cutting will be easier and more aesthetically pleasing.

SQUIDBITS

In Thailand, dried squid is sold from street carts. The bodies are clothespinned to rows of line strung over the cart.

To serve, the squid is briefly toasted dry over little charcoal hibachis. A surprisingly tasty high-protein snack. Try holding them over a gas burner for a few seconds.

In Japan, larger squid is shredded and soft dry-cured in soy sauce, monosodium glutamate, sugar and a variety of spices. The Sarumi, as it is called, is sold like beef jerky here, in plastic. Sarumi can be found in any Japanese foods store.

In South India, boats lay nets in immense semi-circles out from the beach. An entire village of dozens of people drags the nets up onto the beach. Most of the squid are laid uncleaned directly on the sand for drying. After washing and soaking, they are used in curries, often coconut milk based. The texture is somewhat chewy and the flavor full-bodied.

SQUID NUTRITION

The composition of 100g edible portion:
- 68 g water
- 18 g protein
- 1.5 g fat
- 1.7 g carbohydrates
- 92 calories

Depending on your taste, anywhere from 50% to 95% of weight of an uncleaned squid is edible.

WHAT'S IN A NAME?

China: Yao
Indonesia: Tjumi-tjumi (Chew me, chew me)
Japan: Ika
Philippines: Pusit
Thailand: Pla Muk
Vietnam: Muc
Italy: Calamari
Sweden: Kalmar
Norway: Blekkspruter
Greece: Kalamarakia (Com. "Kalimera"—Hello, Good day!)
France: Encomet, Calamar
Holland: Pijinktvis
Germany: Tintenfisch, Kalmar
Portugal: Lula
Brazil: Lula
Russia: Kal'mar
Spain: Calamares
Ancient Rome: Lolligine

OTHER USES AND PREPARATIONS

Chitin is extracted from the quills or backbone of the squid for use in the manufacture of soft contact lenses.

In Thailand, 1 to 2 inch long squid are used whole in spicy relishes.

Sepia, which is cuttlefish ink, has been used for thousands of years as ink for writing and drawing.

SELECTING SQUID

Squid is a paradox in the cooking world: a food that is at once extremely perishable, requiring fastidious selection and handling to preserve its unique delicacy, and a food that is extremely stable, that can always be made to taste good.

This apparent contradiction is easily resolved. For dishes of low flavor intensity, such as found in the European and Japanese cuisines, the squid must be extremely fresh. If it has been frozen, it must have been very fresh when it was frozen and should be thawed just prior to use.

For dishes of high flavor intensity, such as found in Southeast Asia, the extra flavor of slightly older squid, with its characteristic "fishiness" is acceptable or even desirable.

Fresh fresh squid that has never been frozen is a real treat if you can find it. *De rigeur* for raw dishes, it is firm but not flabby, has a mild odor, has iridescent green and blue highlights, and dark freckles on a translucent ivory-to-gray ground. Squid that's this fresh has a lovely subtle undercurrent to its flavor reminiscent of abalone. The skin adds a special quality to the flavor when it is completely fresh. The eggs are especially tasty as well. Slightly older squid becomes increasingly purplish and limp. Extreme flabbiness or yellowish dry looking patches (freezer burn) are to be avoided, as is an overly fishy odor.

Unlike most seafood, squid freezes extremely well, if frozen properly. It is much more widely available than you might imagine, tucked away in obscure corners of supermarket freezers. Unfortunately, it is more difficult to assess the quality of frozen squid without thawing it. Look for light, not over purplish color, and absence of freezer burn. We recommend buying squid in the frozen state if you are not planning to cook it immediately. You can thaw one and three pound packages overnight in the refrigerator, or in about half an hour in cold water.

In recent years, a variety of pre-cleaned squid products have become more widely available. Patties of the Mexican *Dosidicus gigas* or Grande Calamari are found in chain supermarkets. As these squid are larger and tougher, the flesh is tenderized on a Swiss Steak meat needler or tenderizer. We do not personally find this form of calamari to be as succulent as the *Loligo sp.* from off our coasts. However, the convenience of cooking may be worth loss in flavor.

Other small scale operations market other forms of squid, which can be quite good. Unfortunately, it can be difficult to evaluate how carefully stock has been handled and rotated when it is wrapped in impermeable plastic. Independent stores who are knowledgeable and conscientious about what they carry are your best bet.

Note also that very small squid take proportionately longer to clean than larger ones.

CLEANING SQUID

The most formidable obstacle to cooking calamari that most people face is cleaning. None of the pre-cleaned forms of squid are ever as good or as delicate as absolutely fresh squid cleaned right before cooking, so it is definitely worth your while either learning to clean them yourself, or teaching someone else. Luckily, cleaning squid is very easy.

Nothing in a squid tastes bad. In Spain, Thailand, and Greece, people often do not bother to clean them at all. They merely discard the hard beak and eyes and the stiff quill when they come across them while eating with no more ado than we make about the tail of a prawn. If the squid are too large a mouthful whole, simply grasp the tentacles and pull them along with the attached innards free from the body. Chop coarsely and cook, with or without removing the transparent quill. If your squid are very fresh, I doubt you will be disappointed with your results.

If you wish to clean them further, the easiest and fastest way is to cut the tentacles above the eyes and pop out the chickpea-sized beak. If you are saving the ink sac, remove it before cutting the tentacles. Then slit open the side of the body. Scrape off the viscera with a reversed knife blade. Flip the body and scrape off the skin the same way. If you wish to score or cross-hatch the bodies *à la orientale*, flip it again. Scoring needs to be done from the inside of the body for the pieces to hold together correctly.

INK SACS & TENTACLES

With a little patience and lots of squid, you can collect a sizeable quantity of the silvery ink sacs.

Needless to say, the sacs are exceedingly messy if you break them. Consequently, some care is required to remove them intact.

For dishes that highlight the ink sacs themselves, you may wish to freeze small quantities as you generate them until you have saved enough.

Squid tentacles may be too exotic for some of your guests. Serve them the mantles cut in squares—masquerading as generic protein—and save the tentacles for yourself.

HOW TO CLEAN SQUID

1

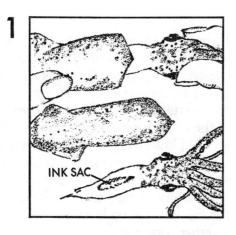

If you are saving the ink sac, remove it *before* cutting the tentacles. The sacs are quite messy if you break them. Consequently, some care is required to remove them intact. Pull out the head, and whatever insides are attached. The silvery ink sac comes out with the head and the tentacles. Carefully remove the sac and set it aside.

2

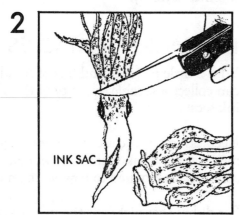

Cut the head and tentacles just in front of the eyes. Some recipes request that some skin be peeled from the legs. You may do this now or later.

3

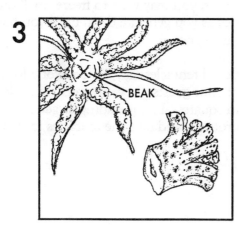

Pop out the hard, round chickpea-sized beak, located where the tentacles come together. Some recipes cut the tentacles shorter, ". . . so they aren't so scary," was one explanation.

4

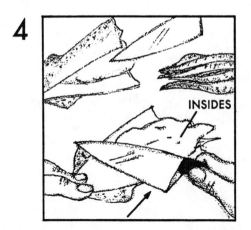

INSIDES

For flat "steaks," strips, scored pieces, and other preparations which don't use a whole body, the easiest and fastest way is to slit open the side of the body and scrape off the viscera with the knife angled away from you as shown.

5

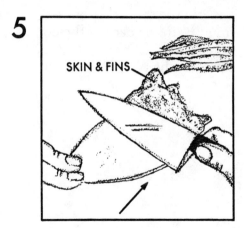

SKIN & FINS

Flip the body and scrape off the skin and fins in the same way.

6

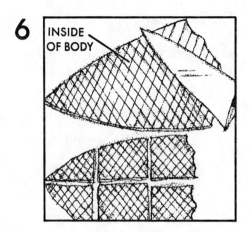

INSIDE OF BODY

If you wish to score or cross-hatch the body pine-cone style, flip it again. Scoring needs to be done on the inside of the body so that the pieces hold together and curl correctly. Be careful to avoid cutting through the body when scoring. Scores may be quite close together or as much as 1/4 inch apart, depending on personal preference.

7 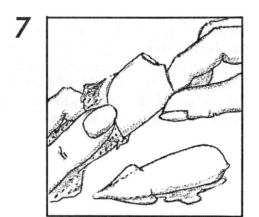 If you are keeping the bodies whole for stuffing or rings, peel the skin from the body, either by pulling off the fins and continuing to remove the rest of the skin; or, if the fins are to be saved for certain recipes, keep them in place when you peel off the skin.

8 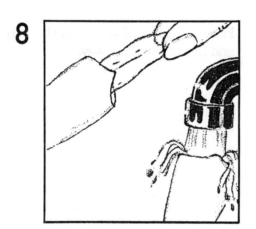 Remove the thin cellophane-like spine from the inside back of the body. Squeeze out the rest of the insides and rinse out the body cone in running water.

9 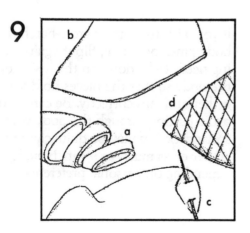 The body may be prepared for cooking in these and other ways described in the text: (a) rings, (b) opened flat, (c) used as a container for stuffing (recipes vary on how the body is to look when it is stuffed), and (d) scoring. There are also various preparations of raw squid for different kinds of sushi.

SALADS &
COLD DISHES

NIGIRI SUSHI
(JAPAN)
Vinegared rice and squid "sandwiches"

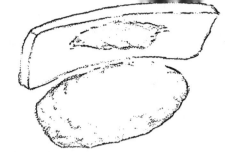

DRESSING

1/4 cup rice wine vinegar
4 Tbs. sugar
2 Tbs. salt
2 Tbs. sake
1/2 tsp. MSG (finished dish is OK if this is omitted, but something of the spirit will be missing)

Bring vinegar, sugar, salt, sake to boil in enamel or stainless steel pan. Add MSG.

1 1/2 cups "sushi rice" or unconverted white rice
2 cups water
2-inch square kombu (dried or fresh kelp; rinsed)

Combine rice and water. Let soak 30 minutes. Add kombu, bring to boil, stir, cover, simmer 10 minutes. Turn heat to minimum, let simmer another 5 minutes. Let rest, covered, 5 minutes off the heat. Discard kombu. Spread rice on large non-metallic platter. Pour on all but 2 Tbs. of the dressing, mix quickly and thoroughly. Fan rice to cook quickly. Use when cooled to room temperature.

2 1/2 lbs. fresh squid bodies, cleaned, in pieces about 3″ × 1 1/2″
1 Tbs. wasabi powder (green horseradish powder) mixed with 1 Tbs. cold water, set aside to rest 15 minutes

Mix reserved sushi dressing with 1/4 cup cold water. Dip fingers into this mixture, pick up a tablespoon or so of the rice, shape into oblong. Smear a bit of the wasabi paste on a squid square, then cram the rice and squid together so the squid covers the top of the rice.

Serve with soy sauce and pickled ginger.

Many other configurations of raw calamari and rice are found, some with nori seaweed.

6 dozen

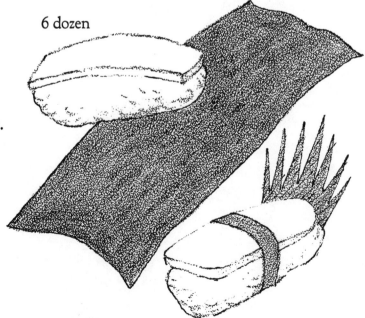

FISKESALAT MED PEPPERROTSAUS
(NORWAY)

Calamari salad with horseradish sauce

2 lbs. squid, cleaned, bodies in fat rings,
  tentacles whole or halved
4 Tbs. freshly grated horseradish or prepared
  horseradish
2 cups sour cream
2 Tbs. finely chopped onion
1 tsp. white vinegar, if using fresh
  horseradish
3 Tbs. finely chopped fresh dill
1 Tbs. salt, to taste
dash white pepper, to taste
1 medium head lettuce
2 hard-boiled eggs, sliced
3 tomatoes, wedged

Simmer calamari in water to cover until
firm but not tough, about 1 minute. Drain
and chill. Mix together horseradish, sour
cream, onion, half the dill, salt, and pepper.
Check the balance; add vinegar if needed.
Fold in calamari. Arrange on lettuce. Deco-
rate with eggs and tomatoes, strew with
remaining dill.

6 servings

NUTA-AE
(JAPAN)

Chilled squid in miso sauce marinade

1½ lbs. squid, cleaned, bodies in rings,
tentacles halved
1 bunch scallions, cut into 1½" lengths
½ cup light miso (shiro miso)
1 Tbs. rice wine vinegar or white wine
vinegar, to taste
1 Tbs. sugar, to taste
1 tsp. mustard, powdered, mixed with hot
water to make paste, let rest 15
minutes
2 egg yolks (Method II), beaten
½–1 cup sake

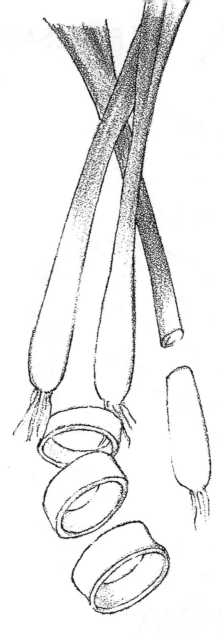

Cut squid into small pieces. Blanch in boiling water very quickly, 15–20 seconds. Rinse under cold water, drain. Blanch green onions in salted boiling water for 1 minute. Rinse under cold running water and drain.

METHOD I
Blend together sugar, miso, vinegar, sake, mustard to consistency of mayonnaise. Fold in squid.

METHOD II
Simmer together sugar, miso, sake 20–30 minutes. Remove from heat, quickly beat in yolks to thicken, then cool bottom of pan in ice water, beating to cool dressing. Mix in vinegar and mustard. Fold in squid.

Serve at room temperature.

6–8 servings as side relish/salad

LULA IMOJO
(BRAZIL)
Marinated spicy squid and shrimp salad

3 lbs. squid, cleaned in rings or scored, with tentacles
6 bay leaves
1 onion, chopped, some coarse, some fine
1/2 tsp. black pepper, fresh ground, to taste
1 cup fish or prawn stock; best with shrimp shells simmered in and strained out
1 cup shrimp, fresh or frozen, shelled and de-veined, shells saved for stock
2 tomatoes, chopped
1 red bell pepper, chopped
1 green bell pepper, chopped
4 Tbs. fresh parsley, finely chopped
1 tsp. chili water, to taste
1/2 cup lemon juice
1/2 cup olive oil
2 Tbs. tomato paste

Simmer stock with onions, bay, and pepper. Poach shrimp and squid until just done, strain out and chill. Concentrate down the stock and strain. Chill or at least let cool.

Mix everything together. Not too much stock. Balance flavors. Let marinate.

6 servings

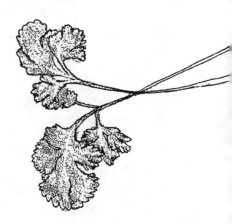

CALAMARI-KIWI SALAD

(USA)

Squid poached in marinade with kiwi fruit

3³/₄ lbs. whole small squid, cleaned as directed for strips; or 1¹/₂ lbs. cleaned mantles
2¹/₂ cups dry white wine
³/₄ cup regular-strength chicken broth
2 large cloves garlic, minced or pressed
³/₄ tsp. sugar
1 medium-size red bell pepper, stemmed, seeded, and cut into thin strips
¹/₃ cup olive oil
¹/₂ tsp. freshly ground pepper
2 or 3 kiwi, peeled and sliced
watercress sprigs

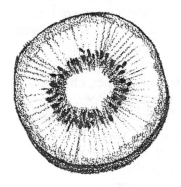

If squid mantles are whole, cut each open with a sharp knife (left). Cut crosswise into ¹/₂-inch-wide strips.

In a 10- to 12-inch frying pan, combine wine, broth, garlic, and sugar; bring to a boil over high heat. Add squid; return to boil and poach until opaque, about 20 seconds. Lift out with a slotted spoon; set aside. On high heat, boil liquid down to ¹/₂ cup, uncovered.Cover; chill liquid and squid separately.

Blend liquid, squid, red bell pepper, oil, and pepper. Spoon onto a platter. Garnish with kiwi and watercress.

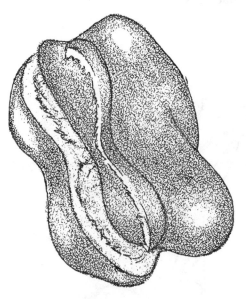

4–6 servings

YAM CHOMPHU
(THAILAND)
Tart fruit squid salad/side relish

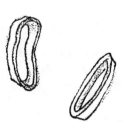

1 lb. squid, cleaned, bodies in thin rings,
    tentacles in small pieces, simmered
    until firm but not tough, drained
    and chilled
2 large tart apples, or 2 mangoes; or 1 small
    pineapple, peeled and finely sliced
$1/2$ cup thinly sliced, simmered, chilled pork
2 Tbs. soaked, very finely chopped dried
    shrimp *or* 4 Tbs. cooked shrimp,
    peeled and deveined
juice of 1 lemon *or* 3 Tbs. tamarind water
$1^{1}/_{2}$–2 tsp. sugar
3 tsp. fish sauce, or more to taste
very slight amount of chili water, to taste

Simmering or soaking the various meats in
the same water, then making tamarind water
with the same water will conserve the maximum flavor. In any event, toss all ingredients
thoroughly together.

6 servings as relish

INSALATA DI MARE
(ITALY)
Marinated squid salad

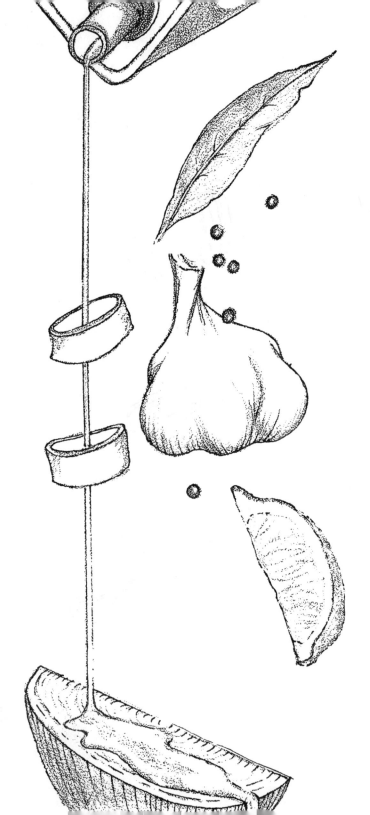

2 lbs. squid, cleaned, bodies in rings,
      tentacles whole
1 cup olive oil
3 cups onions, thinly sliced
1/4 cup garlic paste, or sliced cloves of garlic
1/2 tsp. thyme, dry, crumbled
3 bay leaves
8 peppercorns
1 tsp. salt, to taste
1 cup wine vinegar, preferably white
1/2 cup white wine
1/2 cup water
3 Tbs. lemon juice, to taste

Heat oil. Add onions, garlic slices, thyme,
bay, peppercorns. Fry until onions are transparent, not brown. Add vinegar, wine,
water. Bring to boil, then simmer about 20
minutes. If garlic paste is used, fry it briefly
at this point. Let cool some, so the squid
won't overcook when added.

Add squid, 1 Tbs. lemon juice, cover and
refrigerate at least 24 hours.

To serve, adjust salt-tart balance with salt
and more lemon juice, slightly drain squid.

4–6 servings

MUSHIDORI TO IKA NO GOMAZU
(JAPAN)

Squid-vegetable-chicken platter with sesame-soy-sake dip

1 lb. squid, cleaned, bodies opened flat and halved or quartered, tentacles halved or quartered

2 chicken breasts, boned, skinned, cut in one inch squares

8 strands *wakame* (a variety of dried seaweed), soaked in warm water 30 minutes, rinsed, cut into bite-sized pieces, or substitute soaked hijiki seaweed

1 cucumber, thinly and broadly sliced

1 carrot, thinly and broadly sliced

1/2–1 cup other vegetables, decoratively sliced: radishes, daikon, asparagus, jicama, etc.

2 Tbs. sesame seeds or black sesame seeds, toasted

1 tsp. garlic paste, to taste

1 tsp. soy sauce, to taste

2 Tbs. mirin (sweet cooking sake) or 2 Tbs. sake plus 1 tsp. sugar

3 Tbs. mayonnaise

1/2–1 tsp. togarashi-ko (Japanese hot pepper condiment), or substitute cayenne with a little MSG

Using a Japanese or Chinese steamer, or improvising one, steam the chicken breast pieces. The steaming water may have sake added. When the chicken has steamed about 4 minutes, add squid and continue steaming another 3–4 minutes until they are both just cooked. Remove chicken and squid and let cool. Grind sesame seeds in mortar and pestle or spice grinder. Or mix sesame seeds with a little of the steaming liquid (save the rest for another use), the garlic, the soy sauce, and the sake, and blend until the seeds are pulverized and the sauce thickens. Stir in the other ingredients and adjust texture and taste. Sauce should be fairly delicate. Arrange vegetables, chicken, and squid beautifully on a platter. Serve with sauce on side.

3–4 servings

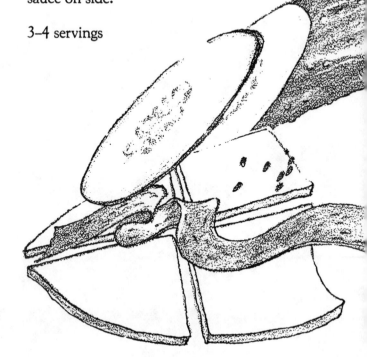

MUSHIDORI TO IKA NO GOMAZU

(JAPAN)

Squid-vegetable-chicken platter with sesame-soy-sake dip

RELISHES &
CONDIMENTS

GNAH PEE GOUNG
(BURMA)

Burmese hot squid relish

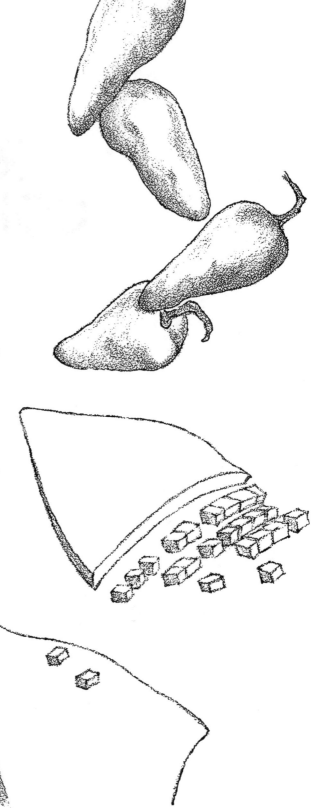

1 lb. squid, cleaned, finely diced; older squid
     is OK, if not preferable to fresh, for
     this dish
$1/2$ cup peanut oil
$1/2$–1 cup thick fresh chili water
$1/2$–1 Tbs. salt, to taste
1 Tbs. rice wine vinegar (optional)

Fry everything except the vinegar over
moderately high heat until all liquid evaporates and the oil separates out. Add a couple
tablespoons of water and continue frying
until mixture is again dry. If necessary to
balance the flavor, stir in the vinegar. This
relish is extremely concentrated and hot.
Minute amounts, $1/4$ teaspoon or less, are
used as a tingly "tongue toucher" with
Southeast Asian dinners. If made with a fair
amount of salt and vinegar, this relish will
keep indefinitely when refrigerated.

SAMBAL TJUMI-TJUMI
(INDONESIA)
Hot calamari-shrimp paste condiment

1 lb. squid, cleaned, very finely diced
2–4 Tbs. fermented shrimp paste (trassi,
    blachan, kapi)
1–2 medium onions, very finely diced
1/2 cup peanut oil
2–4 Tbs. dry crushed chilis, or cayenne
2–4 Tbs. garlic paste
0–2 Tbs. sugar (optional)
1/2–2 Tbs. paprika
2–5 Tbs. rice wine vinegar

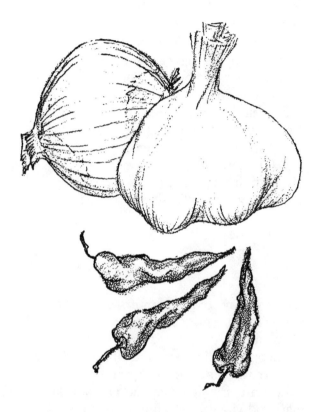

Fry shrimp paste in oil over high heat, preferably in a wok. Break it up with a spatula as it fries and stir constantly. When it sizzles and starts to bubble and melt, after a minute or so, add the onions. Fry the onions until richly browned, adding a tablespoon of water from time to time to prevent burning. Stand back from the stove and add the cayenne. The fumes coming off the mixture about now are going to make you wonder whether the whole project is worth the trouble. Stir-fry the cayenne a minute or so, then add the garlic paste, squid and sugar. Burned onions and garlic are very bitter, so carefully fry the garlic until dry and lightly browned, adding a little water from time to time as necessary. Stir in the paprika, more if you have used less chili. Stir in the rice wine vinegar to taste. If the relish is too hot to taste the flavor balance, mix a small amount with rice. Keeps indefinitely covered and refrigerated.

Language note: Tjumi-Tjumi is plural for squid as it appears in an earlier standardized form of Bahasa. The current form, still pronounced approximately "choo-mē–choo-mē," is cumi-cumi. This expression of plurality is commonly written cumi[2] or tjumi[2]. The squaring of a singular creates the plural, and saves space for the typesetter and the sign painter. We are using the older spelling (tjumi-tjumi) because the pronunciation is more readily understood.

MACHLI ACHAR I
(INDIA)
Calamari pickle

1½ lbs. calamari, cleaned, bodies in fat
        rings, tentacles halved or quartered
4 Tbs. peanut or light sesame oil
1 Tbs. opium poppy seeds, or substitute
        dark poppy seeds
1 Tbs. black mustard seeds
1 tsp. crushed red pepper or cayenne (2 tsp.
        paprika for a milder version)
3–5 Tbs. garlic paste
½–1 tsp. fresh ginger, thinly sliced
2–4 fresh green chilis, sliced, or use fresh
        chili water
½ cup vinegar
½–1½ tsp. salt

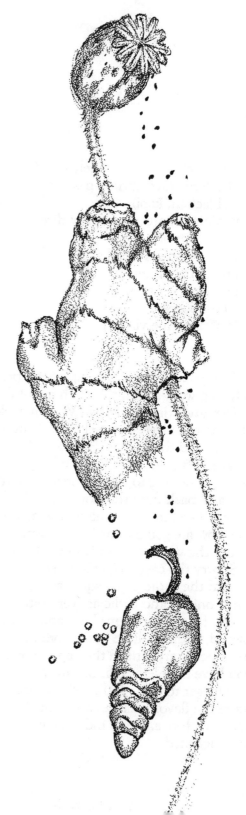

Grind poppy seeds and mustard seeds together in spice grinder or mortar and pestle. Or blend oil, poppy seeds, mustard seeds, red pepper, garlic paste, and ginger slices in blender with enough water to process. In either case, fry all ingredients except calamari and vinegar for a minute or so, until the aromas are heightened and the oil begins to separate from the spices. Add vinegar and simmer for about 10 minutes. Stir in calamari. For maximum flavor, refrigerate for a couple of days before serving.

This relish will keep several weeks under refrigeration.

2–3 cups

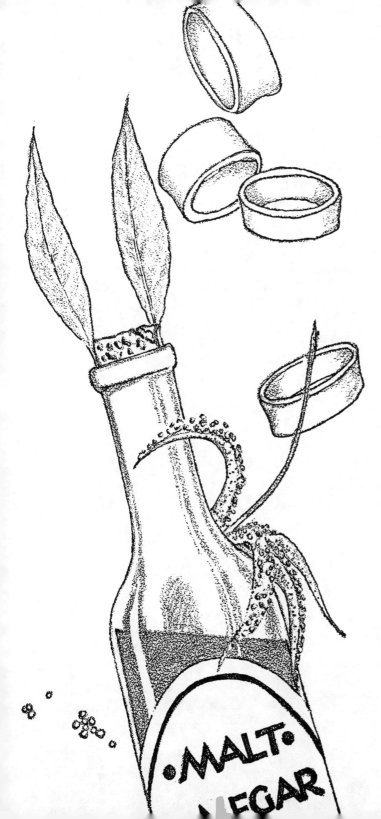

MACHLI ACHAR II
(INDIA)
Calamari chutney

1½ lbs. squid, cleaned, bodies in fat rings,
      tentacles in pieces
salt, about ½ cup
2 Tbs. peanut oil
½ medium onion, diced fine
1 Tbs. ground mace
1 Tbs. fresh ginger slivers
½–1 Tbs. freshly ground black pepper
½ cup chopped raisins
2 bay leaves
3 cups vinegar, malt or distilled
2 cups sugar

Mix calamari with salt. Let stand 6 hours.
Rinse and drain. Fry onion in oil until transparent. Add other ingredients and simmer
until a thick syrup is formed.

Stir in squid, adjust salt balance, pour into
sterile jar with tight-fitting lid. Marinate 1
month before using. Will keep at least 4
months.

5–6 cups

SERUNDENG KATJANG TJUMI-TJUMI
(INDONESIA)

Crispy calamari-coconut condiment

1 coconut, shelled, finely grated
1/2 tsp. turmeric
1/8 tsp. ground cumin
1/4 tsp. ground white pepper
1 tsp. salt
1/4 tsp. *trassi*, fermented shrimp paste, or
    substitute anchovy paste, crumbled
0–1 Tbs. sugar or brown sugar
1/4 cup tamarind water
1/2 medium onion, cut into very thin, even
    slices
1/2 cup vegetable oil
1/2 cup peanuts, coarsely chopped
1 tsp. ground coriander (optional)
4 curry leaves, or substitute 2 bay leaves
1/2 lb. squid, cleaned, finely diced

Preheat oven to 400 degrees.

Combine coconut, turmeric, cumin, pepper, salt, sugar, trassi, coriander, and curry leaves. Mix well. Stir in tamarind water and 2 Tsp. oil. Mix well, again. Spread mixture on baking sheet and toast it in the oven, stirring occasionally.

Meanwhile, heat up the remaining oil in a wok or skillet, wok much preferred. Fry the calamari until crisp. Drain. Fry peanuts until light golden. Drain. Fry onions until light brown and crisp, stirring constantly and being careful not to burn them. Drain.

In about 45 minutes, the coconut will be golden brown and crisp. Let cool to room temperature, stir in the peanuts, calamari, and onions. Discard the curry leaves.

This is used as a side relish to elaborate South Asian dinners. It keeps indefinitely if sealed and refrigerated, so it may be worth making extra.

2–3 cups

GADO-GADO SAUCE
(INDONESIA)
Spicy peanut coconut milk sauce

We serve this with all our Indonesian dishes at India Joze. It is basically peanut butter gone to heaven. Its richness goes especially well with the leanness of calamari dishes in general. This sauce may be frozen, but does not keep well under refrigeration.

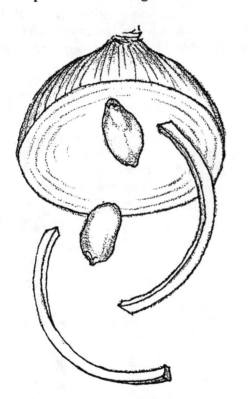

3 Tbs. peanut oil
$1/2$ tsp. trassi, hard shrimp paste (optional, but adds authentic flavor body)
1 medium onion, diced fine
2 tsp. fresh ginger slivers
2 tsp. fresh garlic paste
$1/8$ tsp. ground bay leaf
1 Tbs. molasses or brown sugar to taste
2 cups coconut milk, thin is fine
$2/3$ cup peanut butter, smooth or crunchy
3 Tbs. tamarind water
1 tsp. fresh chili water, to taste

Sauté trassi, if used, until it crumbles and smells strong. Sauté onions until transparent.

Add ginger, garlic, bay leaf, sugar or molasses, and coconut milk. Simmer 10–15 minutes. Whisk in peanut butter and tamarind water. Sauce should now be about the consistency of heavy cream. Add more peanut butter or coconut milk (or water) as needed.

Add chili water and adjust the seasoning. Simmer 5 minutes, stirring to prevent sticking.

SAMBAL GORENG SETONG
(MALAYA)
Chili-fried coconut milk-squid relish

1½ lbs. squid, cleaned, bodies in rings,
    tentacles halved
2–3 Tbs. peanut oil
1 red or yellow onion, finely chopped
2 Tbs. Brazil nuts or almonds
½ tsp.–1 Tbs. dried hot chilis, seeded if a
    less hot result is desired
½ tsp. *trassi* (fermented shrimp paste)
½ tsp. lemongrass powder
4 Tbs. tamarind water
1 Tbs. brown sugar, or less, to taste
1 tsp. paprika
1 tsp. grated lemon peel
½–1 cup coconut milk (optional)
1 Tbs. lemon juice (optional)

Two separate dishes here with basically the same ingredients. The first is a side dish/relish, usually very hot, with tough, chewy squid morsels, eaten in small quantities. The second is more properly a "curry"; a saucy, more centerstage dish.

Blenderize peanut oil, onion, nuts, chilis, and trassi to smooth paste, adding water as necessary for efficient blending. Preheat skillet or wok, fry spice paste and lemongrass over high heat until brown, stirring constantly, adding water a little at a time as needed to prevent burning. The mixture will sputter and spatter; protect self, or turn down heat (but this just prolongs the agony). Turn down heat, add tamarind water, sugar, paprika, and grated lemon peel.

Now, the two variations:

I   Cut squid finely. Add squid, cook uncovered, stirring constantly until sauce looks oily, dry. This keeps a long time as a relish.

2 cups

II   Use slightly less chili in initial spice paste. Add coconut milk (first and second extracts). Simmer 15 minutes or so without squid, until sauce coats spoon lightly. Then add squid, cook very briefly, 10–15 seconds, *or* simmer 15–20 minutes. Serve as curry.

4 servings

SIMMERED & SOUPS

SHIKUMCHEE-TAENG-JANG-KUK
(KOREA)
Squid-tofu soup with spinach

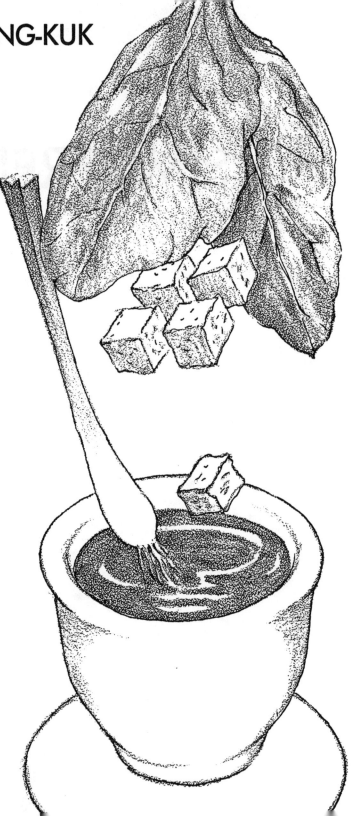

2¹/₂ cups beef stock
1 cake tofu, preferably fresh and soft, cut in
    cubes
¹/₂ lb. squid, cleaned, bodies in thin rings,
    tentacles in pieces
¹/₄ lb. spinach, well-washed and coarsely
    chopped
¹/₂–1¹/₂ tsp. garlic paste
1 Tbs. Korean bean paste or dark miso
2 green onions, finely chopped in rings
¹/₂ tsp. MSG (optional, but authentic)

Combine all ingredients but tofu. Heat,
gently stir in tofu, simmer a minute or so.

2–4 servings

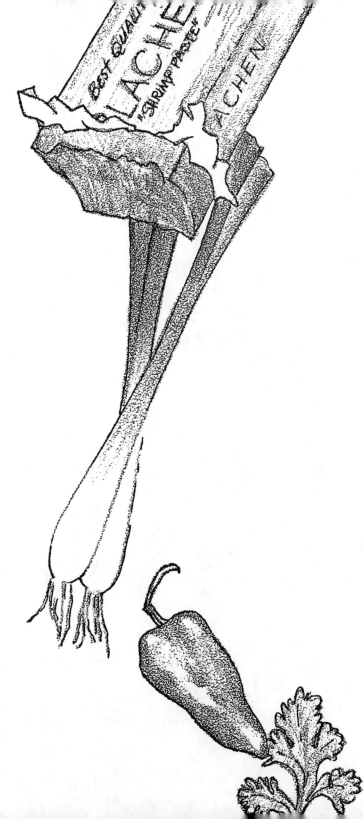

PLA TOM YAM
(THAILAND)
Spicy tart calamari soup

1½ lbs. squid, cleaned, bodies in rings, tentacles whole

2 tsp. laos powder

4 citrus leaves, or lime leaves, torn into pieces

1 stalk fresh lemongrass, cut into 1″ lengths, crushed, or peel of ½ fresh lemon and 1 tsp. dried lemongrass

4 cups water

½ cup lemon juice to taste

2–4 tsp. sambal trassi (substitute any Southeast Asian fried, fermented shrimp paste condiment)

1–2 Tbs. fish sauce, to taste

1–2 Tbs. chopped green onion

1–3 Tbs. chopped fresh coriander leaves (cilantro)

Boil water with laos, lemongrass (or peel), and citrus leaves for a couple of minutes. Add sambal trassi, fish sauce, and squid. Simmer briefly. Add lemon juice, remove from heat, adjust taste balance. Garnish with coriander, green onion, and, if desired, sliced fresh red chilis.

4–6 servings

TJUMI-TJUMI SMOOR
(SUMATRA)
Squid braised in sweet tomato-soy sauce

1½ lbs. squid, cleaned, bodies in rings,
      tentacles whole
1 medium diced onion
1 Tbs. garlic paste
½ tsp. ground cloves
½–1 tsp. ground white pepper
¼–½ tsp. ground nutmeg
2 medium tomatoes, diced
1 Tbs. soy sauce
dash–4 tsp. laos
½–1 tsp. molasses or brown sugar
¼–1 tsp. fresh chili water
2–3 Tbs. peanut oil

Sauté onion in oil until transparent. Fry
garlic briefly. Add other ingredients, reserving one tomato. Simmer 10–20 minutes,
until tender. Add reserved tomato. Adjust
flavor balance.

2–4 servings

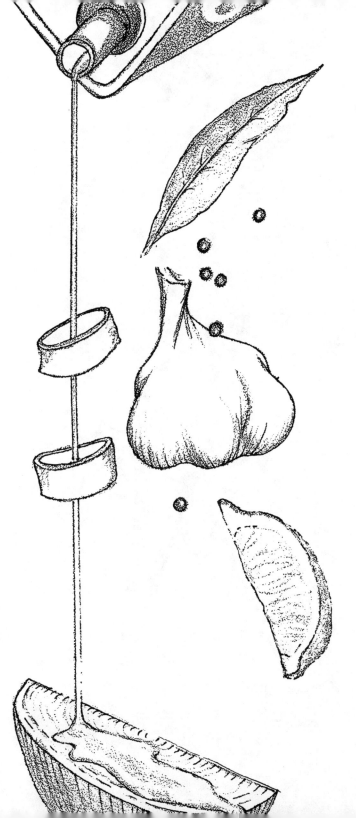

CREOLE CALAMARI
(USA)
Squid-vegetable stew with gumbo filé

3 lbs. squid, cleaned and cut into rings
4 Tbs. olive or vegetable oil
1–4 Tbs. garlic paste
1 medium onion, coarsely chopped
1/4–1/2 cup slivered ham
1 red bell pepper, chopped
1 green bell pepper, chopped
1 cup canned diced tomatoes
4 bay leaves
2 cups fish stock or clam juice
salt
black pepper
cayenne
1–2 tsp. gumbo filé powder
1 tsp. lemon juice (optional)

Fry onion and ham in oil until onion becomes transparent. Add garlic and fry until lightly browned. Add peppers, tomatoes, bay, stock, salt, cayenne, and pepper. Simmer 10–15 minutes. Add squid, simmer 2–3 minutes until just done. Off the heat, stir in the gumbo filé. Adjust seasoning with salt, cayenne, and lemon juice and serve.

6 servings

CALDEIRADA
(PORTUGAL)
Squid-vegetable stew

2 lbs. squid, cleaned, bodies and tentacles in
   large pieces
1/4 cup olive oil
2 onions, sliced
1 tsp. cumin
1/2 tsp. black pepper
6 bay leaves
1/2 bunch parsley, chopped
3 Tbs. garlic paste, or coarsely chopped,
   peeled cloves
1 cup white wine
2 cups stock or water
2 potatoes, chopped
2 carrots, chopped
1 Tbs. salt, to taste
2 cups tomatoes, may as well use canned
1/2 cup pimentos, red bell pepper, or a little
   paprika (1 Tbs.)
2 Tbs. fresh coriander leaves (cilantro),
   chopped, to taste
1 Tbs. lemon juice, to taste

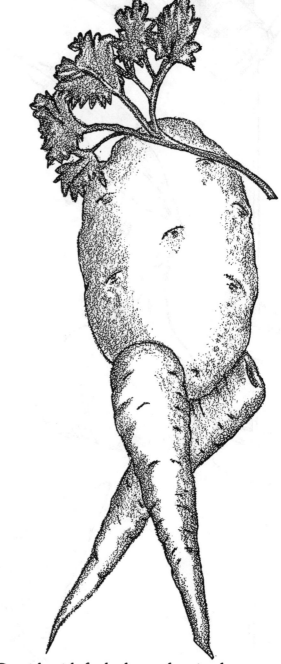

Heat olive oil, add onions, cumin, bay leaf,
potatoes, carrots. Fry until onions color
lightly. Add salt, garlic, parsley. Fry a while
longer. Add wine, tomatoes, pimentos,
squid. Simmer until tender, at least an hour,
depending on sexual activity of squid immediately prior to their demise.

When squid is tender, balance tartness with
a little lemon juice (should not be very tart).

Garnish with fresh chopped coriander.

8 servings

VATAPA
(BRAZIL)

Brazilian calamari stew with nuts and coconut milk

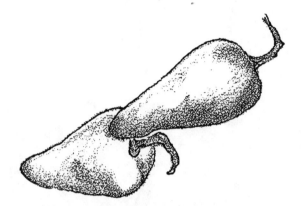

4 lbs. squid, cleaned, bodies in large pieces,
    tentacles whole
1/2 cup olive oil
2 large onions, diced
1–2 Tbs. garlic paste
2 cups diced tomatoes, canned are fine
1/2–3 Tbs. fresh coriander leaves, (cilantro),
    chopped
1 tsp. salt

Gently sauté onions until transparent in
olive oil. Lightly fry garlic. Add tomatoes
and enough water or bottom coconut milk
to give a thicker-than-soup consistency. Add
coriander and salt. Simmer about 10 minutes. Add calamari and simmer over lowest
possible heat, stirring occasionally, for
maybe 5 minutes. Let cool. Strain out squid,
reserve liquid.

SAUCE

1–2 cups top or mixed coconut milk (de-
    pending how much sauce is desired)
1/4–1/2 cup peanuts, lightly roasted or fried
1/8–1/4 cup almonds or cashews, lightly
    roasted or fried
2 Tbs. dried shrimp or 1/2 lb. peeled, de-
    veined raw shrimp, sliced
1/4 cup sweet French bread, preferably
    slightly stale
1–2 Tbs. fresh ginger, chopped

1/4–1 tsp. crushed chilis or cayenne or
    1/2–11/2 tsp. fresh chili water
lemon juice to taste
salt to taste
dendê oil, or substitute olive oil simmered
    with annatto seeds or paprika
fresh coriander leaves (cilantro) to garnish

Grind coconut milk, nuts, dried shrimp (if
using fresh, reserve until later) bread, ginger,
and chilis with the reserved cooking liquid
in a blender or food processor. Add more
coconut milk or nuts as needed to make a
smooth paste as thick as heavy cream. Simmer this sauce 10 minutes or so, until it is
reduced and thickened more than you desire. Add the squid and the raw shrimp if
you are using it, adjust the flavor with
lemon juice, salt, and chili water. Stir in
dendê oil. Garnish with fresh coriander.
Serve with rice or plain boiled hominy.

8 servings

EGG & CALAMARI

SQUID EGG FOO YUNG
(CHINA)

Chinese squid omelet cakes

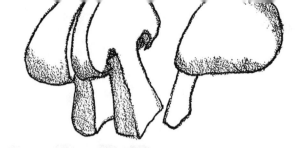

3/4 lb. squid, cleaned, bodies in 1/4" dice,
     tentacles in small pieces
1/2 cup fresh bean sprouts
1/2 cup fresh mushrooms, cut into 1/4" dice
1 Tbs. dried shrimp, soaked and ground
     into a paste (optional)
4 Tbs. peanut oil
3 eggs

FOO YUNG SAUCE

3/4 cup chicken stock, fresh or canned
1 Tbs. soy sauce, the better, the better
1/2 tsp. salt
1 Tbs. cornstarch dissolved in 2 Tbs. stock
     or water

Bring sauce ingredients to a boil, stirring
constantly. When thick and clear, reduce
heat and keep warm.

Wok or stir-fry squid and shrimp paste over
high heat with 2 Tbs. oil for half a minute
or less. Beat eggs in a bowl, stir in mushrooms, bean sprouts, and squid-shrimp.

Heat 1 Tbs. oil in wok or skillet, add 1/4
cup of the egg mixture, cook undisturbed
over moderate heat for about a minute, until
lightly browned, then flip and cook the

other side about a minute. Repeat this procedure until egg mixture is used up. Pour
sauce over each of the pancakes and serve.

4 servings

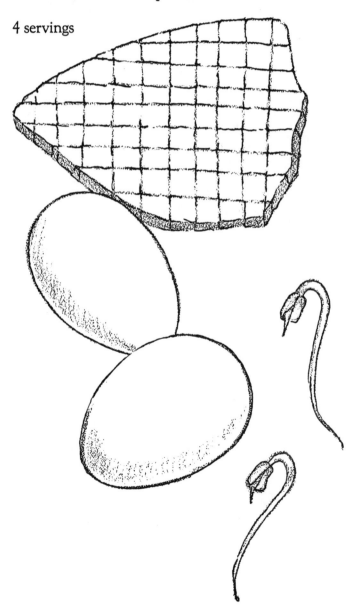

OMELETTE AUX CALMARS
(USA)
Herbed cheese-squid omelet

¼ cup finely diced, cleaned squid
¼ cup white wine
2–3 Tbs. fresh herbs, finely diced (any combination of basil, tarragon, chives, parsley, chervil, dill)
3 Tbs. butter
5–6 eggs beaten with 2 Tbs. warm water
salt to taste
freshly ground pepper to taste
½ tsp. fresh lemon juice, to taste
2–4 Tbs. grated cheese (Gruyère, sharp cheddar, Parmesan, or combination)

In a small skillet, concentrate down the wine and 1 Tbs. of the butter until the wine is almost gone. Add squid and herbs, salt and pepper to taste. Sauté until squid is barely cooked. Balance flavor with lemon juice. Keep warm.

In 10-inch skillet or omelet pan, heat butter over medium heat until it just starts to brown. Raise heat to high, add eggs. With spatula, rubber scraper, or deft flicks of the wrist, keep moving and lifting the cooked egg mass so the uncooked egg flows out and gets cooked. When all is almost set, spread with the calamari filling and cheese, fold over and serve. Rely on the stored heat in the eggs to continue cooking the omelet once it is removed from the heat. The flavor is much more delicate if the eggs are not overcooked. Overcooked eggs can be somewhat redeemed by garnishing with sour cream.

2 servings

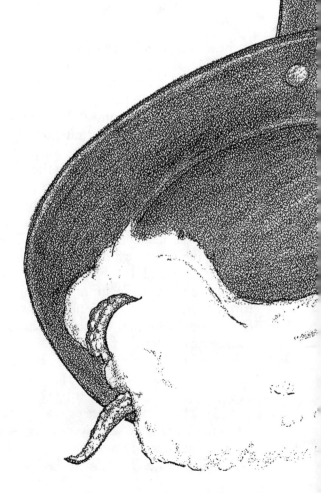

CALAMARI QUICHE
(USA)

PASTRY

8 Tbs. butter, chilled and cut into
    $1/4''$ dice, or 6 Tbs. butter
    and 2 Tbs. lard
$1^{1}/_{2}$ cups all-purpose flour
$1/4$ tsp. salt
3–4 Tbs. ice water

Preheat oven to 400 degrees.

Rub the butter, salt, and flour together with your fingertips or a pastry blender until the mixture looks like cornmeal. Work quickly to prevent the mixture warming up and becoming oily. Pour 3 Tbs. ice water over the mixture and toss lightly together. The particles should just barely adhere enough to form a ball; add a little more water, if necessary. Refrigerate the dough for an hour, if you have time. Then, on a lightly floured surface, pat the dough out into a circle. Roll it out to about 12–13″ diameter with a rolling pin or wine bottle, lifting, flouring, and turning the dough to prevent sticking. Drape the dough over the rolling pin to transfer it to a 9-inch pie pan. Press it into the sides and bottom of the pan, being careful not to stretch the dough. Patch any splits or gaps with trimmings, wetting the patch to make a firm bond. Flute or scallop the edges as you will. A $1/2''$ layer of beans will prevent the bottom from buckling as the crust bakes. Bake the crust in the lower half of the oven until set, about 10 minutes. Then remove the beans and bake a few more minutes until very lightly browned.

FILLING

1 lb. calamari, cleaned, bodies in rings, tentacles in pieces
2 large red onions, thinly sliced
3 Tbs. butter
$1/4$ tsp. freshly ground pepper
$1/4$–$1/2$ tsp. garlic paste
$1/4$ cup white wine
$1/2$ tsp. salt, to taste
$1^{1}/_{4}$ cups half-and-half or milk
4 eggs, well-beaten
3 Tbs. green onions, finely chopped
and either:
    2 Tbs. olives, pitted ripe, chopped
    (optional)
              or
    1 Tbs. parsley, very finely
    minced
1 Tbs. *fresh* herbs, finely minced
    (tarragon, sweet basil, chives,
    oregano, thyme, marjoram,
    savory)
              or
    4 Tbs. pimento, sliced
$2/3$ cup grated cheese, more or less to taste
    (medium cheddar or a mixture of
    Parmesan and Gruyère are both
    good)

Preheat oven to 350 degrees.

Sauté onions with butter over moderate heat until transparent and limp, but not brown. Add wine, garlic, salt, and pepper and continue cooking until all liquid evaporates. Remove skillet from heat, let cool a minute, stir in the calamari. Patch any cracks in the baked pastry crust with a flour-water paste. In a mixing bowl, mix together the half-and-half, eggs, green onions, and olives or herbs or pimento. Stir in calamari-onion, and salt and pepper to taste. Pour into pastry crust, sprinkle with the cheese, and bake in the middle of the oven until set, about 25 minutes. The quiche will be creamier if it is not baked until it starts to rise and puff. Serve hot or cold.

4–6 servings

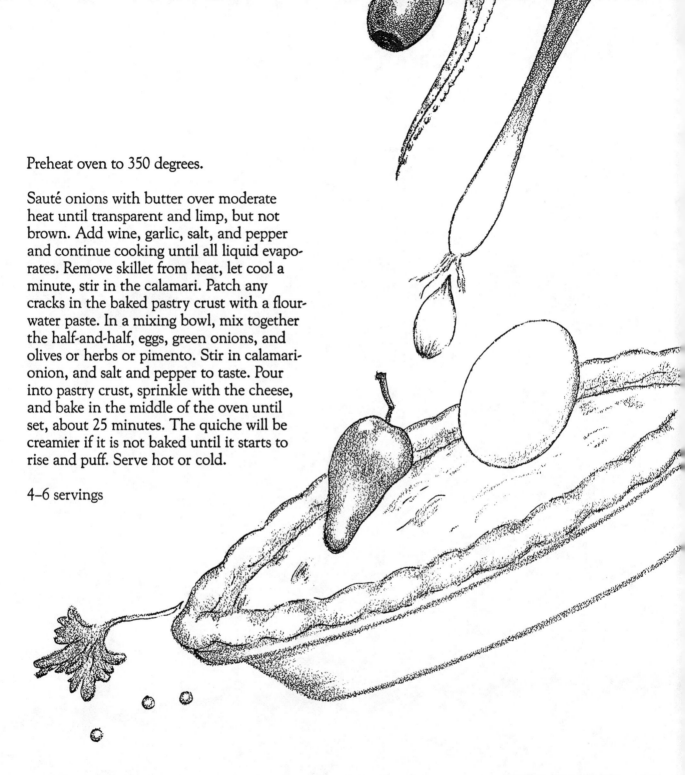

STUFFED

MUC NHOL THIT
(VIETNAM)
Pork-stuffed squid

12 squid, preferably small, about 1¹/₂ lbs.
  before cleaning
¹/₂ lb. ground pork
2 Tbs. garlic
¹/₄ cup shallots or whites of scallions, finely
  chopped
¹/₂ tsp. black pepper, to taste
1 Tbs. fish sauce, to taste
¹/₂–1 Tbs. sugar, to taste
¹/₂–1 tsp. salt, to taste

Wash and drain squid well. Chop tentacles
finely, mix well with other ingredients. Stuff
squid ²/₃ full. Close with toothpicks, if you
wish. Steam over high heat in oriental
steamer, or shallow-fry about half an hour.

Serve with rice steamed dry with no salt,
with greens and herbs, and carrot-radish
pickle.

VEGETABLE PLATTER

lettuce leaves
fresh mint
fresh coriander (cilantro)
thinly sliced cucumbers

CARROT-RADISH PICKLE

Very thin flower-shaped slices in equal parts
vinegar (distilled or rice wine) and sugar.
Salt to taste. Bring to boil, let cool.

4 servings

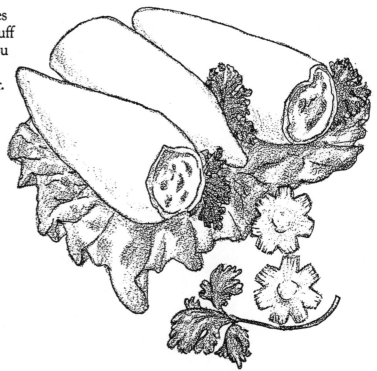

CALAMARI RIPIENI
(ITALY)
Calamari stuffed with ricotta

12 large squid bodies, cleaned; reserve
    tentacles for another use
1 cup ricotta cheese
4 Tbs. Parmesan or Romano cheese
4 Tbs. finely chopped parsley
1/2 cup bread crumbs
1 large or 2 small onions, diced
2–3 Tbs. olive oil
1/2–1 Tbs. garlic paste, to taste
dash ground pepper, preferably freshly
    ground

SAUCE

2 cups canned tomatoes, preferably Italian
    plum (fresh will do, but need more
    cooking and even so will give less
    body to the final sauce)
1/2 cup red wine
1 cup stock, preferably beef or veal (or 1/2
    cup more wine and 1/2 cup water)
2 bay leaves
salt and pepper to taste

Sauté onions in olive oil until transparent.
Add garlic and fry lightly. Stir in other ingredients. Adjust taste balance. Stuff squid
mantles about 2/3 full. Close with toothpicks. Arrange snugly in baking dish. These
steps can be done up to a day ahead of time.

Simmer sauce ingredients together until
thick, breaking up tomatoes. The sauce will
not taste too special at this point; it gets a
lot of flavor from the squid juices. Spread
sauce over stuffed squid. Bake in moderate
oven (350 degrees) 30 minutes or so.

3–4 servings

IN LOLLIGINE FARSILI
(ANCIENT ROME, AFTER APICIUS)
Stuffed squid in rich sauce, ancient Roman style

STUFFED SQUID

1 dozen squid, cleaned, bodies whole,
      tentacles finely chopped
1 cup sweet French bread, in small pieces
1 small diced onion, preferably red
3 Tbs. olive oil
3 Tbs. parsley, finely chopped
1/4 cup mushrooms, sliced
salt and pepper, to taste

Sauté onion in olive oil over medium heat
until transparent. Add mushrooms, parsley,
and squid tentacles; sauté until mushrooms
wilt. Add bread and sauté a couple of minutes. Adjust seasoning. Stuff squid 2/3 full.
Arrange in skillet. They should fit snugly.

SAUCE

1 cup wine, white or red
1/2 tsp. lovage, ground (aromatic herb avail-
      able at large herb stores)
1/2 tsp. ground white pepper
1/2–1 Tbs. fresh coriander leaves (cilantro),
      finely chopped
1/2–1 tsp. celery seeds, ground
1 Tbs. honey
2 Tbs. wine vinegar
1/2–1 Tbs. fish sauce
2 Tbs. olive oil
2–3 egg yolks, lightly beaten
coriander leaves to garnish

Mix ingredients, pour over squid. Bring to a
boil, simmer, covered, over very low heat or
in medium-slow oven for 20–45 minutes.
When squid are tender, drain off liquid into
saucepan. Let cool a little. Whisk in yolks,
then heat, whisking constantly until thick.
Adjust flavor balance. Pour over squid, garnish with coriander leaves.

3–4 servings

KALAMARAKIA DOLMA
(GREECE)

Calamari stuffed with rice, pine nuts, and raisins

2 lbs. squid, cleaned, bodies whole, tentacles chopped
1 cup rice, preferably not brown rice
1 medium onion, finely diced
1 tsp. garlic paste
3–4 Tbs. olive oil
1/4 cup shelled pine nuts, or substitute walnuts
1/4 cup raisins
1 tsp. salt, to taste
1/4 tsp. freshly ground black pepper
1/4–1/2 tsp. ground cinnamon
1 cup white or red wine
1 1/2 cups stock, preferably chicken, or water
1/2–1 Tbs. fresh lemon juice or wine vinegar

Sauté nuts in olive oil in saucepan over medium-high heat until lightly browned. Add onions and sauté further until onions are transparent. Add rice, cinnamon, garlic paste, pepper; and sauté, stirring constantly, until rice grains are coated with oil and translucent. Add salt, 1/2 cup of the wine, and 1 cup of the stock and raisins. Bring to a boil over high heat, then cover and let simmer 15 minutes or so. Let cool, then check the flavor balance. If the dolma are to be served cold, the filling should be a little more tart with lemon or vinegar.

Stuff the squid bodies about 2/3 full. Arrange the stuffed squid in one layer in a skillet. Pour the remaining 1/2 cup of stock and 1/2 cup of wine over them. Add a little more olive oil, if desired. Cover the pan tightly, simmer 10 minutes or so. Serve cold or hot.

4–6 servings

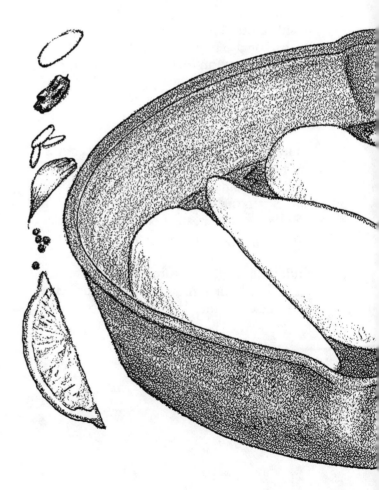

SOUPIES YEMISTA
(GREECE)

On Crete, this is made with cuttlefish

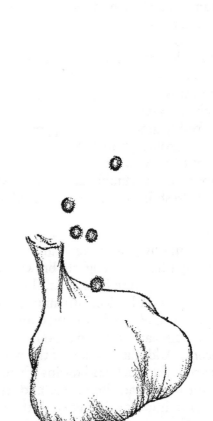

3 lbs. squid, cleaned, bodies left whole, ten-
    tacles chopped
2 lbs. spinach, washed, trimmed and
    chopped if fresh, chopped if frozen
1/4 cup olive oil
2 medium onions, diced
1 tsp. garlic paste
salt
freshly ground pepper
2 Tbs. tomato paste (optional)
1/2 tsp. cinnamon (optional)
1/2 cup dry white wine
1 cup stock, fish or chicken (or water)

Sauté onions in olive oil until transparent.
Add spinach, tentacles, salt, pepper, cinnamon, and tomato paste. Sauté until it waters
out. Strain out spinach, concentrate cooking
liquid over high heat, re-add spinach. Adjust
seasoning slightly on the intense side.

Stuff bodies with mixture, close with toothpicks. Lay bodies in skillet snugly, add wine
and stock. Simmer 15 minutes or so partly
covered.

Serve with French or Italian bread.

6 servings

SAUTÉED

KALAMARAKIA ME SALTSA
(GREECE)

Simmered squid in feta-wine-herb sauce

1 1/2 lbs. squid, cleaned, bodies in rings,
      tentacles whole or halved
1/4–1/2 cup feta cheese
1–2 cups wine (rosé or white)
1/4 cup olive oil
1 onion, diced
2 Tbs. garlic paste
3 Tbs. parsley, very finely chopped
1/2 tsp. black pepper, freshly ground
1 tsp. lemon juice
1/4 tsp. fresh oregano (optional)
2 tomatoes, fresh, diced

Fry onions in olive oil until transparent. Fry garlic briefly; add wine, simmer 10 minutes or so (less if you are pressed for time).

Add feta cheese, pepper, parsley, oregano. Concentrate sauce down to heavier than heavy cream, stirring constantly. Add tomatoes, lemon juice to balance tartness.

Add squid, simmer briefly.

4 servings

CALAMARI FRA DIAVOLO
(ITALY)

Calamari sautéed in wine-tomato sauce

2 lbs. squid, cleaned, bodies in rings,
    tentacles whole
1 large diced onion
1/2–1 Tbs. garlic paste
1/4 cup olive oil
1–1 1/2 cups dry white or red wine
2 cups tomatoes, preferably Italian plum
    tomatoes, fresh or canned, peeled
    and seeded if desired
1–2 Tbs. fresh parsley, preferably flat-leaf
1/4–1/2 tsp. dried oregano
1/4 tsp. cayenne or crushed red pepper
1/2 tsp. salt, to taste

Sauté onions in olive oil over medium-high heat until transparent but not brown. Add garlic, fry a little while after moisture dries off. Add wine and concentrate over high heat until reduced by half. Add tomatoes, parsley, oregano, pepper and simmer over medium heat until sauce is thick. Add squid, simmer another minute or so.

This dish is great served with Italian or French bread and salad
    or
toss this dish with fresh boiled pasta and garnish with grated Parmesan.

4 servings

IN LOLLIGINE IN PATINA
(ANCIENT ROME, AFTER APICIUS)

Squid in pan, ancient Roman style

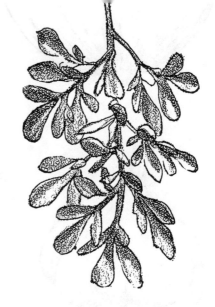

1½ lbs. squid, cleaned, bodies in rings,
    tentacles whole
2 tsp. olive oil
1 tsp. fresh rue (bitter herb; substitute water-
    cress in larger amount, or bitter
    melon, finely chopped)
2 tsp. fish sauce
½ tsp. ground white pepper
1 tsp. honey
½ cup caroenum (red wine concentrated to
    half its volume)
fresh lemon juice to taste

A dish of violent contrasts leading to an
intense balance. Over high heat, stir-fry
everything together, except lemon juice.
Check flavor balance, adjust with pepper,
honey, or lemon juice as needed. Concentrate sauce separately if squid gets done
before sauce thickens.

2–3 servings

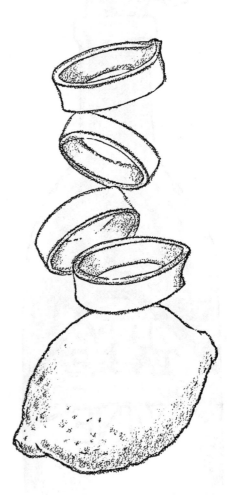

CALAMARI TITI
(ITALY)
Calamari sautéed in caper parsley wine sauce

This dish has emerged as one of the India Joze favorites. Typically, its classic form is a matter of continuing debate. How creamy the final dish should be, and whether tomatoes should be added are the main lines of contention.

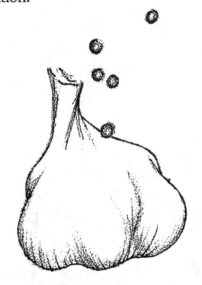

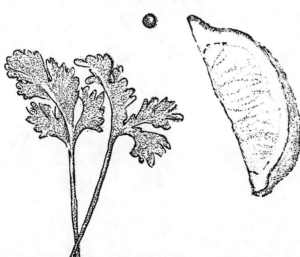

3 lbs. squid, cleaned and cut
1/4–1/2 cup good olive oil
1 medium onion, yellow or red, sliced thin
1 tsp.–1 Tbs. garlic paste
1/2 cup dry white wine
1/4 cup finely cut parsley, preferably the Italian flat-leaf variety
1–4 Tbs. heavy cream
3 Tbs. capers, with juice
salt, to taste
freshly ground black pepper, to taste
1 tsp. fresh lemon juice, to taste
tomatoes, diced, preferably yellow

Heat olive oil in large skillet or wok over high heat. Add onions and garlic paste. Sauté briefly. Add wine, cream, salt, pepper and capers. When sauce is overconcentrated, add squid, parsley and tomatoes. Remove squid when almost done and re-concentrate the sauce if necessary.

Balance seasoning with salt, pepper and lemon juice. Re-combine and serve.

4 servings

BAJJOU CHERMOULA
(MOROCCO)

Squid sautéed in tomato/preserved lemon sauce

1½ lbs. squid, cleaned, bodies in thin rings
    or scored squares, tentacles whole or
    halved
¼ cup olive oil
1½ cups tomatoes, canned, diced (*or* fresh
    and canned)
1 Tbs. paprika
1 tsp. cumin
3 Tbs.–¼ cup parsley, finely chopped
*2 Tbs. preserved lemon peel
¼ tsp. black pepper
1 Tbs. garlic, to taste
⅛ tsp. cayenne (or crushed Moroccan
    chilis, if you can get them)
1 tsp. lemon juice

Fry cumin, parsley, pepper, paprika, garlic,
cayenne. Add canned tomatoes, fry lightly.
Add preserved lemon and enough water to
prevent sticking. Simmer for a few minutes
until sauce is thick.

*Blanch lemon peels 3–5 minutes in boiling
water. Drain. Salt heavily. Put in jars. Cover
with oil. Place in warm location for several
months. Indian lemon pickle may be used
as substitute. If omitted, add ½ finely diced
lemon, including rind.

Right before serving, add squid, fresh tomatoes; balance tartness with lemon juice.
Simmer very briefly.

4 servings

CALAMARI TETZLAFF
(USA)

Squid canapé with raspberries and shiitake mushrooms

2¹/₂ lbs. whole small squid, cleaned so the mantle is left whole; or 1 lb. cleaned mantles
5 large fresh or 5 large dried shiitake mushrooms
2 Tbs. olive oil
1 cup each dry white wine and whipping cream
3 Tbs. raspberry vinegar or lemon juice
¹/₂ tsp. freshly ground black pepper
salt, to taste
30 slices cocktail rye bread, lightly toasted, buttered
fresh or frozen raspberries or very thin lemon slices

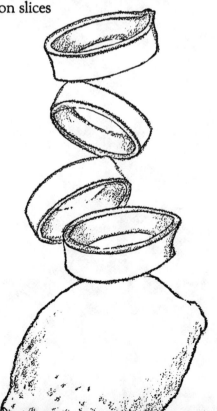

If using whole squid, reserve tentacles for other dishes. Cut mantles crosswise into ¹/₈-to-¹/₄ inch thick rings; set aside. Thinly slice mushrooms. If you use dried mushrooms, soak them first in cold water until soft, about 30 minutes, then cut off and discard stems.

In a 12–14 inch frying pan, warm oil over medium heat. Add mushrooms; cook and stir until fresh mushrooms are just limp or dried ones are hot.

Add wine and cream to pan; bring to a boil. Add squid and cook until just firm, about 2 minutes. Strain out mushrooms and squid. Reserve.

Over high heat, concentrate sauce until heavily reduced. Return squid to sauce along with raspberry vinegar, salt, and pepper to taste.

Spoon mixture onto each rye round, garnish with raspberries and serve at once. Or make ahead and broil briefly to reheat before garnishing.

10 servings

CA RAN CHUAN NGOT
(VIETNAM)

Calamari sautéed in sweet-tart fresh herb glaze

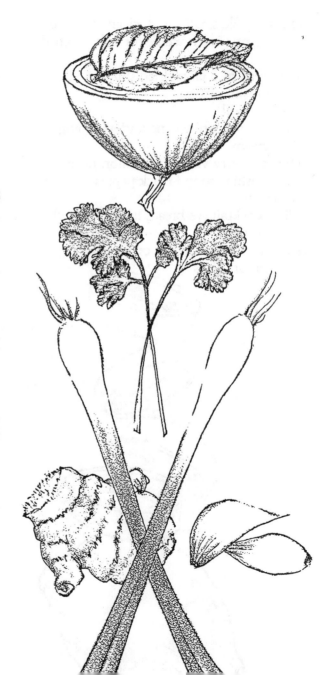

1½ lbs. squid, cleaned, bodies in rings,
    tentacles whole or halved
½–1 cup stock or water
2 Tbs. peanut oil
½ onion, diced
1–2 Tbs. garlic water, to taste
1–4 Tbs. molasses, sugar, or brown sugar, to
    taste
1–2 Tbs. fresh ginger, slivers, to taste
1–2 Tbs. fish sauce (preferably Viet or Thai),
    to taste
2–4 Tbs. rice wine vinegar
1–2 Tbs. fresh coriander leaves (cilantro),
    chopped
1–2 Tbs. fresh mint
1 Tbs. fresh basil (optional)
2–3 Tbs. chopped green onions
1 Tbs. cornstarch mixed with 2 Tbs. water
    (use only as much as needed, do not
    overstarch)

Fry onions and ginger in oil in wok or skillet. When onions are transparent, add garlic and fry briefly. Add stock (or water), fish sauce, rice wine vinegar, sweetener. Balance for sweet-tart-salty. Simmer 10–15 minutes.

Add squid and simmer very briefly. Add fresh herbs. Stir cornstarch slurry into simmering mixture to lightly thicken. Serve with rice.

4 servings

ADOBO
(PHILIPPINES)
Tangy, garlicky braised pork and calamari, Filipino Style

1 1/2 lbs. squid, cleaned, bodies in rings, tentacles whole

1 lb. boneless pork, shoulder or butt, cut into 3/4" cubes (The relative proportion of squid to pork is flexible.)

4 Tbs. peanut oil or other vegetable oil

1/2 cup distilled white vinegar

1 tsp. freshly ground black pepper

1/4–1 cup fresh garlic paste

2–4 Tbs. soy sauce, to taste (The braising stock gets highly concentrated later, so be careful not to oversalt early on.)

1–2 cups chicken stock, pork stock, or water

Brown pork chunks in oil over very high heat in small batches. Pour off oil. Add rest of ingredients except squid and simmer very slowly, being careful that the braising stock is not too salty or tart at this point. When pork is tender, remove and reserve it.

Concentrate braising stock down to syrupy consistency over high heat. Replace pork into sauce. Ideally, let marinate a day or two.

To serve, heat up squid with pork over medium heat for no more than a minute or two. Overcooking or too fast cooking toughens squid. Garnish with tomato wedges and parsley. Serve with plain boiled rice.

6 servings

CALAMARI KICKSHAW
(ELIZABETHAN)

Calamari wok'd with flowers and spices

I doubt that calamari was cooked much during the English Renaissance. If it had been, it would have been used perhaps as a showpiece for the spice-and-flower techniques of the time, like this dish.

3 lbs. squid, bodies scored and chopped, tentacles chopped
3 Tbs. butter
1/2–1 tsp. ground cinnamon
1/4 tsp. powdered mace
1/4 tsp. powdered ginger
1/4 tsp. freshly ground black pepper
1/8 tsp. musk oil (available at herb stores)
1/2 bunch green onions, cut in 1-inch lengths, whites and greens both
1/2 cup frozen concentrated orange juice
1/2–1 tsp. orange or lemon zest
1 Tbs. brown sugar (optional)
3 egg yolks
1/2–1 tsp. fresh lemon juice, to taste
1 cup loosely packed fresh calendula or hibiscus flower petals

Melt butter over high heat. Add spices, green onions, squid, orange juice. Sauté. When squid begins to curl and water out and is almost done, strain off liquid into sauce pan.

Let cool off a little, balance seasoning with salt, pepper, and lemon juice, and a little brown sugar (if you want the authentic intensity of flavor).

Whisk in egg yolks over medium heat until it begins to thicken. Quickly stir in the flowers and squid. Mix well and serve. Note: using egg yolks to thicken a sauce can be very tricky. Undercooked and they are disgustingly slimy, overcooked and they are watery scrambled eggs. Get the mixture out of the pan as soon as it thickens; the heat of the pan will continue cooking the eggs.

6 servings

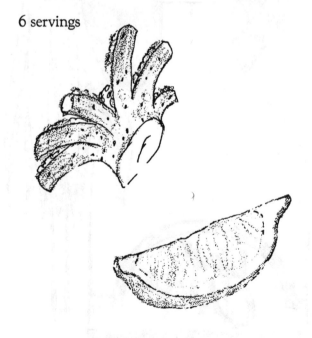

MASAK TJUMI-TJUMI LILANG

(JAVA)

Sautéed squid with fresh basil-nut sauce

2 lbs. squid, cleaned, bodies in strips or
    rings, tentacles halved or whole
2 Tbs. peanut oil
2 Tbs. macadamia or Brazil nuts, preferably,
    or almonds, ground to a smooth
    paste with 4 Tbs. water in blender,
    or in mortar
1/2 bunch scallions, greens only, cut in 1 1/2″
    lengths
1/2–1 Tbs. garlic paste, to taste
dash ground white pepper, to taste
2–4 Tbs. chopped fresh basil (for a different,
    but still special dish, substitute
    chopped fresh mint)
1 tsp. salt, to taste
1 tsp.–1 Tbs. brown sugar (optional, to taste)
juice of 1/2 lemon, to taste
chili water, to taste
1/2 lemon very thinly sliced crossways

Heat oil in frying pan. Throw everything in
and sauté over very high heat, correcting
the taste balance. Adjust heat to produce a
sauce of medium thickness by the time the
squid is cooked, about 30 seconds. Alter-
nately, sauté everything but the scallions,
basil, and lemon slices for a couple seconds,
then strew the basil and scallions on the
top; arrange the lemon slices over, cover and
simmer over very low heat 20–25 minutes.
Drain off liquid, concentrate, check taste
balance, re-apply liquid, serve.

The first technique is more designed for
small quantities and a hot stove. The second
gives more leeway in cooking time, tends to
be more tender, and is more adaptable to
larger quantities and more formal service.

4 servings

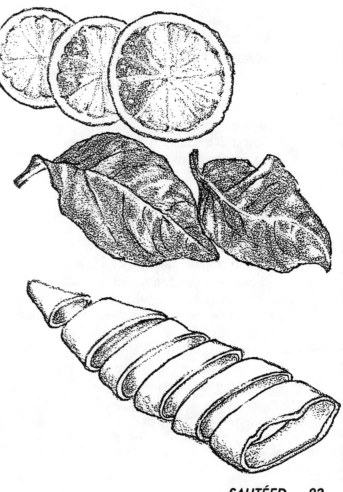

CALAMARES EN MOLE VERDE
(MEXICO)

Squid sautéed in Yucatan tomatillo-pumpkin seed sauce with fresh coriander

2 lbs. squid, cleaned, bodies in rings, tentacles halved
2 cups tomatillos (or green tomatoes),
chopped
2 Tbs. sesame seeds
2 Tbs. pumpkin seeds
1 onion, diced
2 Tbs. garlic paste
3 Tbs. green onions, sliced
1 Tbs. salt, to taste
1 tsp. cinnamon, powder
1 tsp. green chilis, or chili water, to taste
2 Tbs. fresh coriander leaves (cilantro),
chopped, to taste
1 cup chicken stock or water
1/4 cup olive oil
1 tsp. lemon juice, to taste

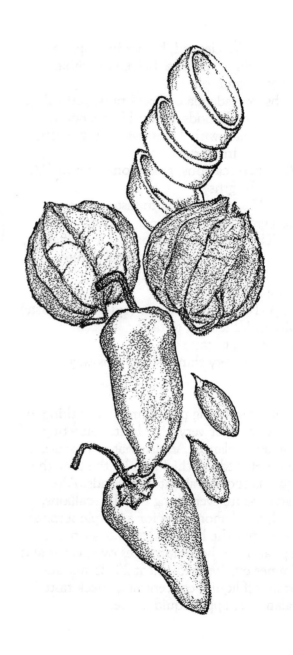

Blenderize sesame seeds, pumpkin seeds,
chilis with water to smooth paste. Fry
onions and cinnamon in olive oil until
transparent, add garlic, fry a little longer,
add nut-chili paste, fry a while. Add stock
or water, olives, tomatillos. Simmer 20 minutes, adding more stock or water as needed
to prevent sticking.

Stir in squid, coriander leaves, lemon juice,
simmer a little while.

Serve with hot tortillas.

4 servings

CALAMARI-GROUNDNUT STEW
(WEST AFRICA)
Squid in spicy African peanut sauce

Serve this stew with cornbread and salsa. This is a recipe that is good with just about any kind of vegetables or meats you have on hand.

2¼ lbs. squid, cleaned and chopped
⅓ cup olive oil
1 cup coarsely diced eggplant
1 small onion, chopped
1 small carrot, chopped
¼–½ tsp. cayenne (optional)
¼–1 Tbs. fresh chili water (optional)
1 Tbs. fresh ginger
1–4 Tbs. garlic paste
½ cup chunk-style natural peanut butter
     (just peanuts)
1 cup chicken stock or water
1 small green bell pepper, chopped or sliced
1 large tomato, cored and chopped, or
     ¾ cup canned tomatoes
2 hard-cooked eggs, quartered
finely chopped parsley
lemon wedges

Fry eggplant, carrot, and onion in olive oil until onion is transparent and eggplant begins to soften. If using cayenne, fry it briefly avoiding the fume inhalation.

Add ginger, garlic, chili water, peanut butter, stock, bell pepper, and canned tomatoes (if used). Adjust seasoning with salt. Sauce should be very thick.

Add squid and fresh tomatoes, simmer 2–3 minutes.

Garnish with eggs and parsley.

4–5 servings

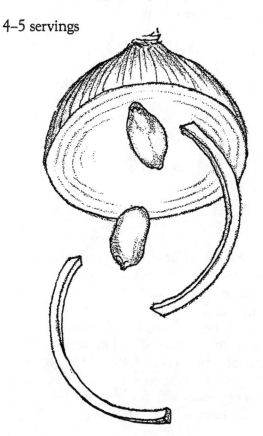

CALAMARS SAUTÉS AUX HARICOTS VERTS ET CHAMPIGNONS

(FRANCE)

Calamari sautéed with green beans and mushrooms

1½ lbs. squid, cleaned, bodies in rings, tentacles halved or quartered
½ lb. green beans, sliced thin and long
¼ lb. mushrooms, sliced
½ cup dry white wine
4 green onions, finely chopped, whites and part of the greens kept separate, *or* 1 small diced onion *or* 2 diced shallots
2 Tbs. butter
1 tsp. garlic paste
½ cup cream
1 Tbs. fresh chives, chopped
1 Tbs. fresh tarragon, chopped, *or* 1 Tbs. fresh chervil, *or* ¼ tsp. fresh coriander leaves (cilantro) and 1 tsp. fresh fennel leaves and 1 tsp. parsley, all chopped
2 egg yolks
½–1 tsp. fresh lemon juice, to taste
1 tsp. salt, to taste
¼ tsp. freshly ground pepper, to taste

Lightly sauté whites of green onions, onion, or shallots in butter. Sauté mushrooms a minute or so, then add garlic, wine, green beans, cream, salt, pepper, and herbs. Cook over high heat. When beans are nearly *à point*, stir in calamari and sauté about half a minute, until nearly done. Strain off the liquid into a saucepan, let cool a little, beat in the egg yolks with a whisk. Replace on medium heat, whisking thoroughly and constantly until sauce thickens heavily. Mix sauce with vegetables and calamari, adjust seasoning, and serve.

2–4 servings

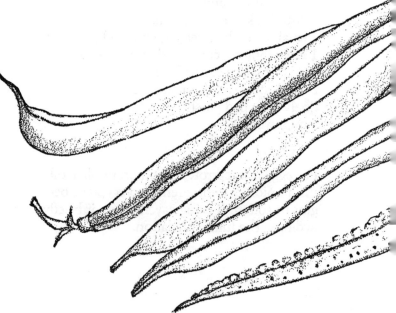

THANDUA MOLI
(SOUTH INDIA)

Calamari in South Indian coconut milk curry

1¹/₂ lbs. squid, cleaned, bodies in rings, tentacles whole

3 Tbs. peanut oil

¹/₂ tsp. black mustard seeds (optional)

1 medium onion, grated or very finely chopped

1 Tbs. fresh ginger, cut thinly across the grain, then into slivers

2–4 Tbs. garlic paste

1–2 tsp. turmeric (optional if other dishes being served are heavy in it)

1 tsp. ground cumin

¹/₂–2 Tbs. fresh chili water, to taste

2 cups thin coconut milk

¹/₂ cup thick coconut milk

¹/₂–1 Tbs. dried mango powder, to taste (substitute tamarind water or fresh lemon juice)

3–4 Tbs. scallions, white parts only, cut into ¹/₂″ lengths, or use peeled pearl onions

0–1 Tbs. chopped fresh coriander leaves (cilantro)

Heat oil with mustard seeds in skillet over medium heat until they sizzle and pop. Quickly add onion to keep seeds from burning, and sauté onions, ginger, turmeric, and cumin until the onions are lightly browned. If the mixture starts to scorch before the onions brown, add water a tablespoon at a time while sautéeing. Then add garlic and chili water, fry briefly. Add thin coconut milk, onions, and mango powder (or tamarind), boil over high heat, stirring constantly, until reduced to about ²/₃ cup. Stir in calamari and thick coconut milk; simmer over very low heat about a minute. Adjust flavor balance. The sauce for this dish is traditionally thin and hot.

3–4 servings

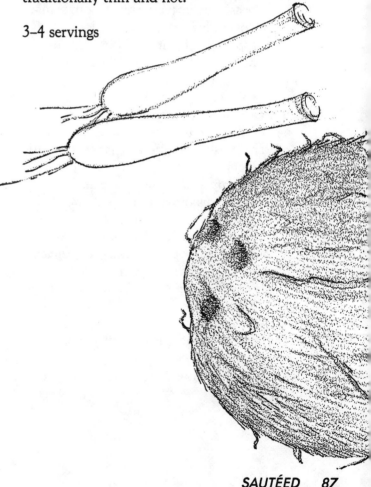

THANDUA KORMA
(NORTH INDIA)
Calamari sautéed in yogurt-vegetable-spice sauce

2 lbs. squid, cleaned, bodies in strips or
    rings, tentacles whole or halved
3 Tbs. ghee or clarified butter
3 Tbs. yogurt
2 Tbs. heavy cream or sour cream
1 cup (more or less) vegetables, large thinly
    sliced of any of the following: zuc-
    chini, onions, green beans, snow
    peas, carrots (very thin slices), cauli-
    flower flowerets, broccoli flowerets,
    asparagus, bamboo shoots, mush-
    rooms, red or green bell peppers
1/4 cup chopped tomatoes and/or chopped
    spinach (optional)
1 tsp. garlic paste, to taste
1 tsp. chili water, to taste
1/2–1 Tbs. freshly ground aromatics, to taste.
    (*Some need to be fried in ghee: black
    mustard seeds, cayenne, cumin, tur-
    meric, cinnamon, cloves—be careful not
    to use too much. Some can just be sim-
    mered in: cardamom, caraway, bay
    leaves, black pepper, fenugreek, fennel,
    fresh ginger slivers, paprika.*)
2 Tbs. ground nuts: almonds, opium poppy
    seeds, cashews, or Brazil nuts
    (optional)
2 Tbs. fresh coriander leaves (cilantro)
    (optional)
1–2 tsp. salt, to taste

This dish can be as elaborate or simple, heavy or light, as you wish. The very incomplete list of Indian aromatics is offered as an antidote to the use of curry powder, a flavoring strategem which soon gets tedious. Any, all, or none of them could be employed.

Fry the aromatics which need it in ghee over medium heat until their smell develops. Quickly, to prevent their burning, add yogurt. Raise heat to maximum, add other aromatics and vegetables (not tomatoes or spinach), salt, cream, and/or nuts. Cook until sauce is very thick and vegetables are almost done, a couple of minutes. Check flavor balance, adding spinach if it seems too sweet-tart and tomatoes if it seems bitter. Add squid, sauté briefly. Garnish with coriander leaves.

4 servings

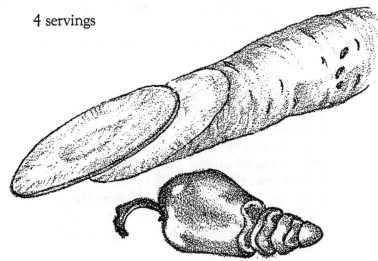

THANDUA KARI
(INDIA)

A rich tomato curry, good very spicy to mild

3 lbs. squid, cleaned and scored, with
  tentacles
4 Tbs. *ghee* or clarified butter or peanut oil
2 tsp. black mustard seeds
1 tsp. ground cumin
1/4–1/2 tsp. cayenne (optional)
1/2 tsp. turmeric
1/4 tsp. ground ginger or 1 tsp. slivered fresh
  ginger
1–2 tsp. garlic paste
1–2 tsp. paprika
1/2 tsp. fenugreek powder (optional)
1/2–1 tsp. ground coriander seed (optional,
  but desirable with spicy versions of
  this dish)
2 medium onions, diced
3 cups tomatoes, diced, canned, or fresh
1 tsp. ground cardamom
salt to taste
1 cup thin coconut milk or water
1–2 Tbs. fresh coriander leaves, chopped
  (cilantro)

Preferably using a wok, fry black mustard
seeds in *ghee* until they start to pop. Stir in
cumin, cayenne (avert face from fumes),
turmeric, and ginger. Fry until the smell
changes. Add diced onions, and fry until
slightly brown. Add garlic, and fry a half a
minute or so. If the spices threaten to burn
at any point, sprinkle in a couple table-
spoonsful of water at a time to moderate
temperature.

Stir in paprika, coriander powder, fenugreek,
cardamom, and salt. Add tomatoes and
coconut milk or water, bring to a boil and
simmer 10–15 minutes. Sauce should be a
little overthick at this point.

Add squid and simmer 3–4 minutes until
done. Adjust seasoning. Serve heavily garnished with fresh coriander leaves.

Serve with rice.

6 servings

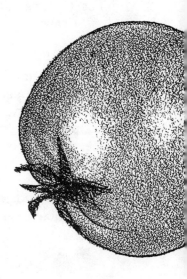

CALAMARI BASELYNNE
(USA)

A colorful squid dish with hazelnut paste

3 lbs. squid, cleaned, bodies scored, tentacles
    halved
3 Tbs. fruity olive oil
1/2 cup straw mushrooms, fresh or canned
1/2 cup asparagus, tips whole, stems sliced
    thin on diagonal
3 Tbs. pimento strips or fresh red or yellow
    bell pepper slices
1/2 cup water or stock
1 Tbs. sherry
salt, to taste
1/2–1 Tbs. garlic paste
1/4 tsp. freshly ground black pepper
3 Tbs. or as needed hazelnut paste made
    from pulverized lightly toasted nuts
1 tsp. fresh lemon juice, to taste
2 Tbs. fresh basil, chopped, and a few whole
    leaves

If using fresh mushrooms, sauté them briefly
in the oil. Then add the red peppers and
asparagus, sherry, stock, garlic, salt, and
black pepper. Sauté until asparagus is almost
done, then add calamari. When squid curls
and waters out, thicken sauce with hazelnut
paste. Add basil. Adjust seasoning with
lemon, salt, and pepper. Garnish with reserved whole basil leaves.

4–6 servings

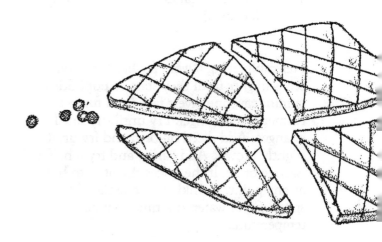

FRIED, DEEP
& SHÁLLOW

SQUID BURGERS
(USA)

calamari patties
bacon drippings, beef drippings, or
      peanut oil
hamburger buns
lettuce
tomatoes
ketchup
mustard
mayonnaise
sliced onions
pickle relish
avocado
cheese
sauerkraut
chili
etc., etc.

Several brands of ground calamari patties
are on the market. These are the ultimate in
calamari convenience, of course, needing
only frying. The type and quantity of oil
used in frying has great effect on the outcome of the dish, as the calamari has so
little oil of its own. The use of a relatively
large amount of oil and high heat will tend
to give a nice crunchy outside layer to the
patty. Any flavor balancing desired can be
accomplished with the various traditional
condiments.

LULA FRITA
(PORTUGAL)
Crisp-fried squid

1¹/₂ lbs. squid, cleaned, bodies in rings,
    tentacles whole
¹/₂ cup olive oil
1 tsp. salt, to taste

Fry calamari over medium heat for 10–15
minutes until crisp. Salt helps draw out the
juices, but be careful not to oversalt, as the
flavor becomes quite concentrated. Drain
on absorbent towelling, salt to taste.

Serve with mayonnaise, commercial or
homemade.

3–4 servings

KALAMARAKIA TIGHANITE
(GREECE)
Squid deep-fried Greek style

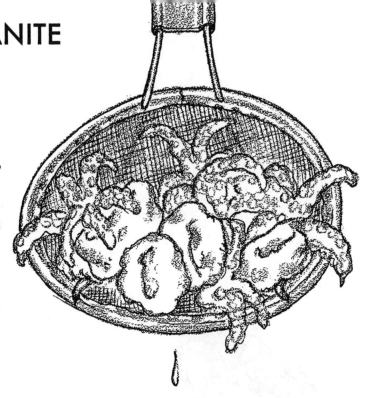

1 lb. squid, cleaned, bodies in strips or rings,
      tentacles whole
1 cup flour
1 Tbs. salt, to taste
$1/2$ tsp. pepper
$1/2$ tsp. paprika (optional)

Drain squid well. Shake in paper bag with
seasoned flour to coat evenly. Let rest a
while. Shake again. Strain off excess flour.
Deep-fry in hot oil (385 degrees) until light
gold. Drain on paper towels.

Serve with lemon wedges or skordalia sauce
(see Kalamarakia Gri-Gri).

4 servings

ABLONETTI
(USA)
Calamari prepared like abalone

1 lb. squid, cleaned, bodies opened out flat
    into calamari "filets"; reserve
    tentacles for another use
2 cups bread crumbs, cracker crumbs, or a
    mixture of the two
1 tsp. salt
$^1/_2$ tsp. black or white pepper, preferably
    freshly ground
3 eggs, beaten
$^2/_3$ cup clarified butter (much preferred) or
    olive oil or peanut oil
2 lemons, cut into wedges

Carefully pound the bodies with the back of
a cleaver, the bottom of a glass, a meat mal-
let, or similar object. The purpose is to get
the tissues to relax, not to beat it to a pulpy
paste; firmness and delicacy are requisite.
Mix the crumbs, salt, and pepper together;
pour onto a plate. Line a baking dish with
paper towels and have it ready in a preheated 250 degree oven.

Heat about half the butter or oil in a large,
heavy skillet over high heat until it almost
smokes. Dip the bodies in the egg, then
dredge in the crumbs, gently shake off the
excess, and lay them out flat in the skillet
without crowding them. A lid that fits inside the skillet can be used to hold them flat
if they tend to curl. Fry on each side no
more than 10 seconds until golden. Drain,
and keep warm on the paper towelling in

the oven while you fry the others, adding
more butter as needed to maintain about
$^1/_2$" frying depth.

Serve with lemon wedges.

2–3 servings

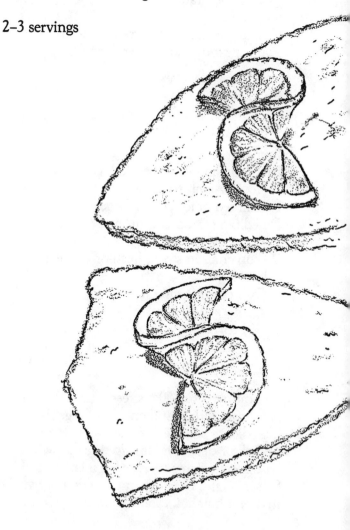

SWEET-AND-SOUR SQUID
(CHINA)

1½ lbs. squid, cleaned, bodies in rings,
    tentacles whole
1 egg, lightly beaten
1 tsp. salt
¼ cup cornstarch
¼ cup flour
¼ cup chicken stock, fresh or canned
3 cups peanut oil or other deep-frying oil

SAUCE

1 Tbs. peanut oil
1 tsp. garlic paste
1 large green pepper, seeded, cut into
    ½-inch squares
1 small red onion, diced large
1 medium carrot, cut into flat matchstick
    sizes
½ cup chicken stock, fresh or canned
4 Tbs. sugar
4 Tbs. red wine vinegar
1 tsp. soy sauce, to taste
1 Tbs. cornstarch dissolved in 2 Tbs. cold
    water

Preheat oven to 250 degrees. Have ready a pan lined with absorbent towelling. Have all ingredients prepared and laid out. Heat oil in wok or deep-fryer to 375 degrees. Mix batter ingredients together in a large bowl. Stir in squid. Deep-fry until golden brown in 2 or 3 batches, carefully dropping squid into oil so that it doesn't clump up. Keep fried squid warm in oven to drain off excess oil.

In wok or skillet, heat oil until it begins to smoke. Stir-fry carrot, onion, and pepper a couple of minutes, being careful to prevent burning. Add garlic and fry a few seconds, then add chicken stock, sugar, vinegar, and soy sauce. Taste for balance, adjust. Boil for about a minute. Give cornstarch slurry a stir, then pour it into the boiling sauce, stirring constantly. When sauce is thick and clear, serve over or beside fried squid.

There are innumerable variations of the classic basic sweet-sour sauce all over the world. Some add ketchup or pineapple juice, some use brown sugar or honey instead of sugar, with some attendant loss of delicacy of flavor. The chicken stock in this recipe is an important part of the Cantonese taste of this dish, but it can be replaced with vegetable stock or water. A finely tuned sense of flavor balance is needed to make this dish successful.

4 servings

IKA TEMPURA
(JAPAN)
Deep-fried squid and vegetables

1 lb. squid, cleaned, bodies in rings, tentacles whole
2–3 cups fresh vegetables (asparagus, mushrooms, carrots, green onions, green beans, bell pepper, snow peas, eggplant, yam, or whatever pleases you, chosen for a balance of tastes, textures, and colors)
1/2 cup flour

BATTER

1 egg yolk
2 cups ice-cold water
1/8 tsp. baking soda
1 2/3 cups flour *or* 1 1/4 cups flour plus scant 1/2 cup cornstarch

DIPPING SAUCES

Ajishio
2 Tbs. MSG   (This amount of MSG may give some diners hot flashes, and other transient uncomfortable symptoms. This sauce should be used as on the borderline between foods and drugs, and is not necessary to the enjoyment of tempura.)
2 Tbs. salt
12 lemon wedges

Ten tsuyu
1/4 cup soy sauce
1/4 cup mirin (sweet cooking sake) or sake with 1/4 tsp. sugar
1 cup ichiban dashi—Japanese dried bonito-seaweed stock
MSG, to taste (optional)
1/4 cup grated daikon or white radish
2 Tbs. grated fresh ginger root

Have all vegetables prepared. Heat oil, preferably peanut oil or peanut oil mixed with sesame oil, in stable wok, deep-fryer, or heavy skillet. Oil must be at least 2 inches deep. For best results, oil should remain about 375 degrees.

Dust squid with flour and shake off the excess. Combine batter ingredients in large mixing bowl. Batter should be quite thin; adjust thickness with flour or water.

Dip one piece of food into the batter at a time, then drop it into the hot fat. Do not crowd the fryer. Skim pieces out after about a minute, when golden brown. Drain on paper towelling and serve immediately, or keep pieces warm on towelling in a slow oven while you prepare the rest. To eat, sprinkle the pieces with lemon juice then dip in the salt-MSG, or dip into spiced soy sauce.

4 servings

PLA MUK TOD
(THAILAND)
Squid fried with garlic and ginger

This is actually two recipes, one with garlic and one with ginger slivers. The sauce would not necessarily be served, but is too good to omit.

3 lbs. squid, cleaned, scored, and chopped, tentacles whole
3 bulbs of fresh garlic, separated into cloves and lightly smashed *or* 1 cup loosely packed fresh ginger cut into match-sticks or slivers
oil for deep-frying
salt

The procedure for this dish is extremely simple: fry the garlic until almost done then fry the squid with it until done. *Or*, fry the ginger and squid together until done. Drain and lightly salt.

However, the nature of your frying setup will dictate how large the batches are you can fry at one time. Avoid crowding the oil, so that the temperature stays between 370° and 390°. In Thailand, this dish is done in a wok and scooped out with a wire strainer.

4 servings

NAM PRIK DAENG
HOT SAUCE

1 Tbs. cayenne
4 Tbs. paprika
1 Tbs. honey or sugar
4 Tbs. distilled white vinegar, or, as needed
1–2 Tbs. garlic paste
1–2 tsp. salt

This sauce keeps indefinitely and is an interesting change from Tabasco.

Mix ingredients together. Adjust flavor balance as needed.

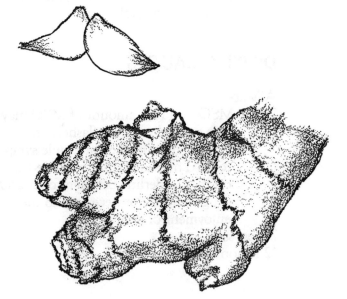

WOK'D

TJUMI-TJUMI ASEM
(JAVA)

Calamari wok'd with tamarind

1 lb. squid, cleaned, bodies scored criss-
        cross, tentacles whole
2 Tbs. peanut oil
1–2 tsp. garlic paste
1–2 tsp. fresh chili water, to taste
½ tsp. freshly ground white pepper
2–4 Tbs. thick tamarind water
green onions, finely chopped, to garnish

Preheat wok over highest heat. Stir-fry everything except tamarind water for about 15
seconds. Add tamarind water, stir-fry until
sauce is desired thickness. Serve with rice.

2 servings

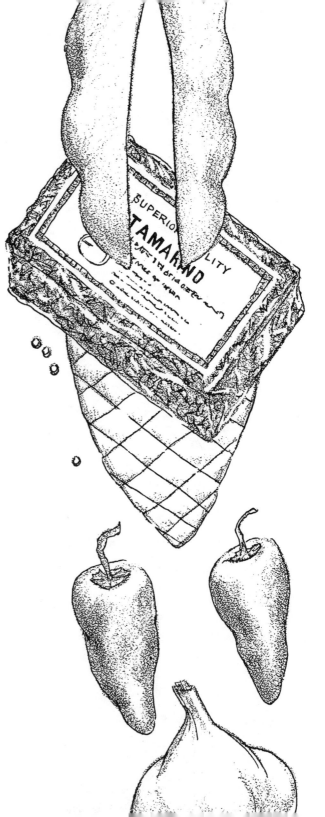

TJUMI-TJUMI TJHA
(CHINA–INDONESIA)
Stir-fried squid with snow peas

1½ lbs. squid, cleaned, bodies in
    checkerboard-scored squares, ten-
    tacles whole or halved
¼–½ onion, diced very fine
2 Tbs. garlic paste
2 Tbs. ginger slivers
¼ cup snow peas
3 Tbs. sherry (or white wine with slightly
    caramelized sugar)
1 Tbs. fresh chili water, to taste
1 tomato, diced
salt and/or fish sauce and/or soy sauce
2 Tbs. cornstarch mixed with water

Fry onions, ginger. Briefly fry garlic. Add
squid, snow peas, tomatoes, sherry, chili
water, and whatever salty substance is used.
Stir-fry briefly (10–15 seconds) over high
heat. Starch lightly to glaze.

Serve with rice.

4 servings

TJUMI-TJUMI SAOS TIRAM
(CHINA–INDONESIA)
Calamari wok'd with aromatic Javan oyster sauce

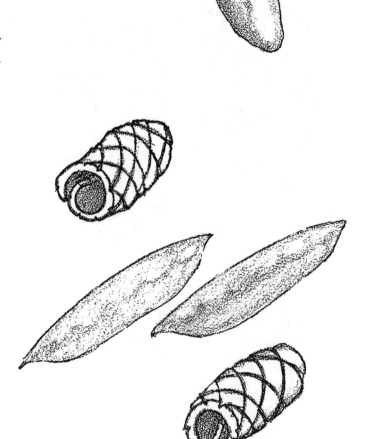

Another favorite at India Joze, the quality
of this dish is dependent on the quality of
the oyster sauce used. If you have access to
more than one type, get one lacking in sugar
and MSG, with more oyster extractives than
water.

3 lbs. squid, cleaned, scored, and cut
2 Tbs. peanut oil or some other neutral
          cooking oil
1/2 cup sliced mushrooms
1/2 cup snow peas, stemmed
1 Tbs. fresh ginger slivers
1/2–1 Tbs. garlic paste
3 Tbs. tamarind water
2 Tbs. oyster sauce
1/2 tsp. freshly ground white pepper, to taste
fresh chili water, to taste

Heat oil in wok over high heat. Add everything. Wok until squid curls. Adjust
seasoning.

6 servings

ZAJIN CHAO XIANYOU
(CHINA)

Stir-fried squid with snow peas and water chestnuts

1¼ lbs. squid, cleaned, bodies opened flat, halved, crosshatched with closely spaced cuts not all the way through, tentacles cut shorter
½ lb. fresh snow peas
6 oz. water chestnuts, fresh or canned, peeled and sliced
2 tsp. cornstarch
1 egg white
1 Tbs. Chinese rice wine or pale dry sherry
1 tsp. salt, to taste
2 Tbs. peanut oil
2 green onions, cut in 2″ lengths
3 slices fresh ginger about 1″ in diameter, ⅛″ thick
1 large peeled bruised garlic clove

Have all ingredients ready. Combine squid and cornstarch in a mixing bowl, then stir in egg white, wine, salt. Let marinate 10 minutes.

Heat oil in wok or skillet over high heat until it just starts to smoke. Add ginger, green onion, garlic; stir-fry until garlic lightly browns, maybe 15–30 seconds. Now that the oil is flavored, remove and discard onions, ginger, garlic. Add squid, peas, water chestnuts; stir-fry about half a minute. Stir the marinade and stir it into the wok. It will thicken into a clear glaze in seconds. Transfer to a heated platter and serve at once.

Several variations: For a hotter, spicier version, sliver the ginger finely, use garlic paste. A dried chili or three can be browned in the oil first before the ginger, and all the spices can be retained in the finished dish. A little hot bean paste (*see under Basic Recipes*) can be added. Or, if you desire more sauce, ½ cup chicken stock can be added after the squid is stir-fried, and a little more cornstarch can be added to the marinade to thicken it up. The Chinese often use dried squid for dishes like these.

2–4 servings

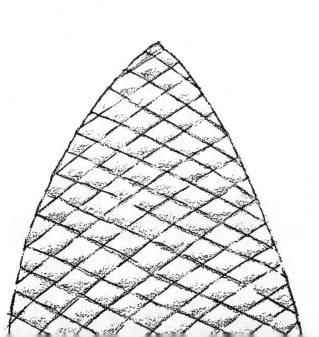

PAD MUN PLA PHET
(THAILAND)
Squid wok'd with hot and spicy fresh basil-anchovy glaze

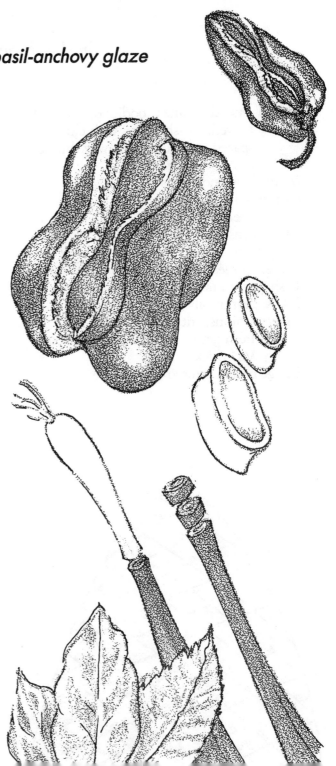

1¹/₂ lbs. squid, cleaned, bodies in rings,
       tentacles whole or tipped
2 Tbs. peanut oil
1 Tbs. fish sauce, to taste
3 Tbs. fresh basil and a little fresh mint (as a
       substitute for holy basil, very rare in
       this country)
3 Tbs. green onions, greens only, in
       1¹/₂″ lengths
¹/₂ tsp. black pepper, freshly ground, to taste
¹/₂ cup slivered green chilis and bell
       peppers—very relative proportions
       according to how hot you want final
       dish
¹/₂ tsp. dried, crushed chilis, simmered and
       soaked in rice wine vinegar (or use
       fresh chili water)

Cook everything together briefly in hot wok
or skillet.

If sauce is too thin when squid is done
(about 15 seconds), remove squid, concentrate sauce separately, add squid.

4 servings

TJUMI-TJUMI TAOTJO
(MALAYA)
Calamari sautéed with vegetables and hot bean sauce

1½ lbs. squid, cleaned, bodies in rings,
    tentacles whole or halved
3 Tbs. sliced bamboo shoots
3 Tbs. thin zucchini slices
3 Tbs. sliced bell peppers, preferably red   or 1–2 cups any
3 Tbs. snow peas, de-stemmed   combination, to
3 Tbs. slivered red onion   taste
3 Tbs. coarsely diced tomato
2 Tbs. peanut oil
2 Tbs. slivered fresh ginger
1 Tbs. finely chopped scallion
¼–½ cup hot bean sauce, or Szechwan
    hot bean paste
garlic paste (optional, to taste)
honey or brown sugar (optional, to taste)
rice wine vinegar (optional, to taste)
chili water (optional, to taste)

Preheat wok or skillet over high heat. Add oil and when it starts to smoke, add the remainder of the ingredients. Stir-fry, adjusting taste balance as it cooks. The mixture should be very dry for the first part of the cooking process, so that the juices which develop during the cooking do not overly thin the sauce. If the sauce is too thin when the squid is done (30 seconds to a minute), strain out the squid and vegetables, concentrate sauce, re-combine. The trick of this dish is the taste and texture balance; much depends on the properties of the hot bean sauce used. In order to have the maximum control and play with this dish, we recommend experimenting with your own hot bean sauce (*see under Basic Recipes*). The sauce keeps almost indefinitely, so the time spent getting the exact balance of hotness-tartness-sweetness-bitterness-saltiness you desire is well spent.

4 servings

OJINGO POKUM
(KOREA)

Squid wok'd with bell peppers

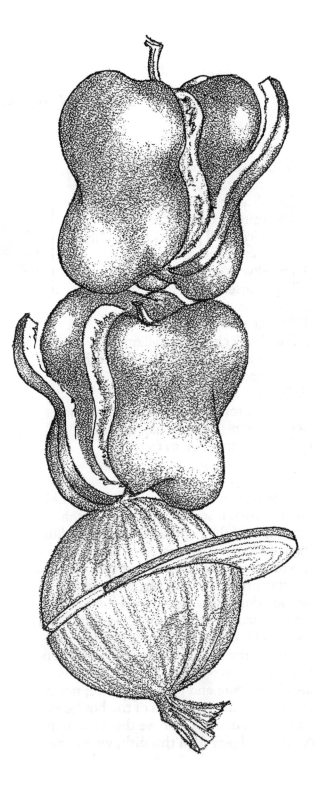

1½ lbs. squid, cleaned, bodies scored in
      crosshatchings, tentacles quartered
3 Tbs. light sesame oil or peanut oil
1 green bell pepper, thinly sliced
1 red bell pepper, thinly sliced
1 small onion, finely diced
1 Tbs. garlic paste
2 tsp. brown sugar
1 tsp. MSG
1 Tbs. *Kochujang*—Korean hot pepper paste
      (or substitute crushed chilis and
      onions fried together in a little oil
      and simmered in a little rice wine
      vinegar)
½–1 tsp. salt

Fry onion in oil. Add other ingredients.
Stir-fry until done. Salt to taste.

2–4 servings

SQUID WITH LOBSTER SAUCE

(CHINA)

Squid prepared with sauce for "Lobster Cantonese"

2 lbs. squid, cleaned, bodies in rings,
    tentacles whole
$1/4$ cup peanut oil
1–2 Tbs. Chinese rice wine or pale dry
    sherry
2 tsp. fermented black beans, chopped
1–2 tsp. garlic paste
$1/4$ lb. boneless pork, cut into matchstick
    sizes, or ground pork
1–1$1/2$ Tbs. soy sauce
1 tsp. salt
$1/4$ tsp. sugar
dash freshly ground pepper
3 Tbs. finely chopped green onions
1 cup chicken stock
2 Tbs. cornstarch dissolved in 3 Tbs. cold
    water
2 eggs, lightly beaten

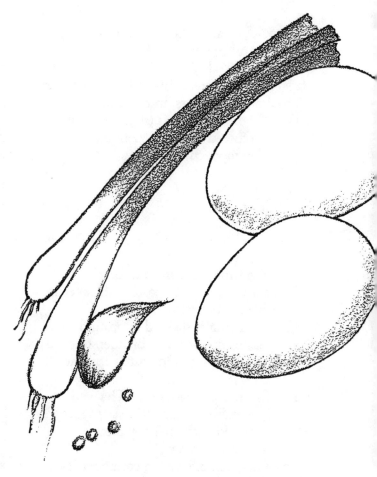

Have all ingredients prepared and at hand.

Preheat oil in wok or heavy skillet over high heat until it begins to smoke. Add pork, fermented black beans. Stir-fry until pork is almost done. Add garlic, stir-fry until lightly browned but not burned. Add calamari, stir briefly, then add wine, soy sauce, salt, sugar, pepper, green onion, and chicken stock. Bring to a boil, then stir in cornstarch. When sauce has thickened and become clear, turn off heat. Then pour beaten eggs slowly over mixture, stirring gently and con-stantly. The finished sauce should be creamy and not curdled; be careful not to overheat at this point. Serve at once.

2–4 servings as main dish, 4–6 as one dish among many

DRAGON SQUID

(VIETNAM)

Squid wok'd with bamboo shoots and Asian mushrooms in piquant fresh coriander-mint glaze

1 lb. squid, cleaned, bodies in thin rings, tentacles whole or halved
2 Tbs. peanut oil
1/2 large onion, preferably red, in thin slivers
3 Tbs. bamboo shoots, in thin, wide strips
3 Tbs. Asian mushrooms (*shiitake* or similar) simmered in water 1/2 hour, de-stemmed, cut in strips

SAUCE

1/2 cup chicken stock *or* mushroom stock *or* water
2 Tbs. rice wine vinegar, to taste
1 Tbs. garlic, ground to paste with water in blender, to taste
1 Tbs. fresh ginger, slivered or ground to paste with water in blender, to taste
1/2 Tbs. chilis, ground to paste with water in blender, to taste
1 Tbs. fish sauce, Vietnam or Thai style preferably, or substitute soy sauce blended with anchovy filet in blender, to taste
1 Tbs. finely chopped fresh coriander leaves (cilantro), to taste
1 Tbs. finely chopped fresh mint leaves, to taste (optional)
1 Tbs. finely chopped green onions
1 Tbs. cornstarch mixed with 2 Tbs. water

Mix sauce ingredients together, checking for balance of saltiness (from anchovy sauce), tartness (from vinegar), hotness (from chilis). Probably the sauce should seem slightly too tart at this point.

Ignite wok, await high temperature, put in oil, then onions, bamboo shoots, mushrooms. Stir briefly. Add squid, stirring enthusiastically and very briefly. Add sauce and herbs. As soon as sauce begins to bubble, stir in just enough cornstarch to lightly thicken.

Serve at once with rice.

2 servings

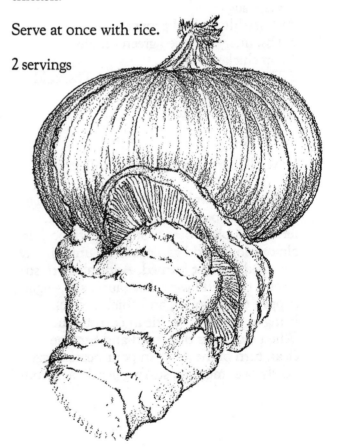

TWICE WOK'D SQUID
(CHINA)

Twice wok'd squid in Chinese brown sauce

3 lbs. whole small squid, scored and
      quartered
3 Tbs. cornstarch
1 egg white
5 tsp. dry sherry
2 Tbs. each: distilled white vinegar, brown
      sugar, and slivered fresh ginger
1 Tbs. soy sauce
3 large cloves garlic, minced or pressed
3/4 tsp. freshly ground pepper
about 2 cups salad oil
2 Tbs. sesame seed
3/4 cup thinly sliced green onions
whole green onions, ends trimmed
lemon slices

In a small bowl, blend cornstarch with egg
white; add squid and set aside. In another
small bowl, combine sherry, vinegar, brown
sugar, ginger, soy sauce, garlic, and pepper.

In a wok or heavy skillet, heat oil until it
almost smokes. Fry squid in 5 small batches,
about 10 seconds for each batch; remove
with a slotted spoon. Drain on paper towels.
Pour off all but 1 tablespoon oil (reserve if
desired for cooking other fish).

Add sesame seeds to pan and cook, stirring,
over high heat until they begin to brown,
about 1 minute. Add sherry mixture and
green onions. Boil 1 minute, stirring; remove

from heat. Mix in squid; spoon onto a serving plate. Garnish with whole green onions
and lemon slices.

4–5 servings

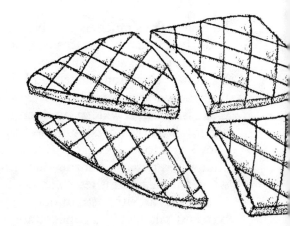

COKED-OUT SQUID
(USA)
Squid in the real thing sauce

1 lb. squid, cleaned, bodies in rings, tentacles whole
2 Tbs. peanut oil
1–2 tsp. slivered fresh ginger
1 tsp. garlic paste, to taste
1/4–1/2 tsp. ground star anise
1 Tbs. beef glaze (1/4 cup strong beef stock concentrated down to 1 T) *or* 1 T beef jerky, pulverized
1 cup Coca-Cola
1 tsp. salt, to taste
1/2–1 tsp. thick fresh chili water, to taste
1 cup thinly sliced bok choy, mostly white part (or substitute 2/3 cup rinsed, fresh mung bean sprouts)
1 tsp. tamarind water, to taste (or substitute lemon juice)
finely chopped green onions to garnish
1 tsp. cornstarch dissolved in 2 t Coca-Cola (optional)

Preheat wok as much as possible. Add oil and when it just begins to smoke, toss in the ginger and garlic, stir-fry no more than 2 seconds, then immediately add the Coke, beef glaze, star anise, salt, bok choy. If the Coke isn't flat, it will fizz up impressively. Be careful. Wok over maximum heat until bok choy starts to look cooked. Add calamari, chili water, tamarind. If the sauce isn't thick when the calamari is ready, about 20 seconds, you can either strain out the vegetables and calamari and concentrate the sauce separately, or you can stir the cornstarch mixture into the wok to thicken the sauce. If you used sprouts instead of bok choy, add them now. Adjust flavor balance. Garnish with green onions.

2–3 servings

NOODLE &
RICE DISHES

NASI GORENG
(MALAYA)
Squid-fried rice

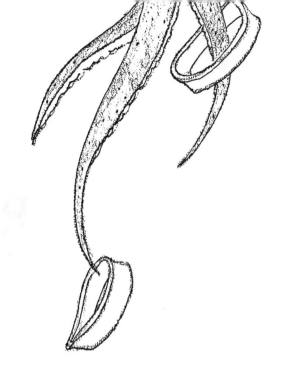

1 lb. squid, cleaned, bodies in rings, tenta-
    cles whole or in pieces
3 cups cold cooked rice
2 Tbs. peanut oil
2 tsp. fresh ginger slivers
1 tsp. garlic paste
1–3 Tbs. fish sauce, or substitute soy sauce
    with ½ tsp. anchovy paste crushed
    into it
1 egg omelet, cooked flat and hard, diced
1 Tbs. dried shrimp, soaked and finely
    chopped *or* 2–4 Tbs. chopped,
    peeled, deveined shrimp

shredded beef ⎤
shredded pork ⎥ any combination
shredded chicken ⎥ of these adding
shredded lobster ⎥ up to ½–1 cup
diced fresh firm fish filet, such ⎥
    as snapper, ling cod ⎦

3 Tbs. daikon, cut into matchstick-sized
    pieces, or bok choy or celery
1 small red onion, slivered lengthwise
½ red bell pepper, or pickled red bell, or
    canned pimento
2 Tbs. chopped artichoke heart, with mari-
    nade (optional)
1 medium tomato, chopped (optional)
1 Tbs. rice wine vinegar (if needed)
4 tsp. bean sprouts
2 Tbs. chopped green onions

Heat oil in wok or skillet over high heat.
Briefly sauté ginger, garlic, and meats, if
used. Add vegetables (which could predomi-
nate in this dish if desired) and squid, stir-
fry a few seconds. Add fish sauce and rice,
wok until rice is hot. Add tomato, bean
sprouts, omelet pieces. Check flavor balance.
Add more fish sauce and rice wine vinegar
if needed. Sprinkle in some water if the dish
is too dry. Garnish with chopped scallions
and roasted peanuts.

This dish is very flexible in its additions and
deletions of ingredients, very quick to prepare. The Vietnamese pickles for which we
have substituted bell pepper and artichoke
hearts would generally be served on the
side, with fresh greens and herbs.

4–5 servings

FETTUCCINE AL TOTANI
(ITALY)

Pasta with squid-ham-wine-Parmesan white sauce

1¹/₂ lbs. squid, cleaned, bodies in rings,
    tentacles in small pieces
³/₄–1 lb. pasta, preferably freshly made
    fettuccine, spaghettini, linguine
¹/₂ cup ham slivers or bacon slivers
¹/₂ onion, finely diced
2 Tbs. garlic paste
1 cup white wine
¹/₂ tsp. black pepper, freshly ground
¹/₂ tsp. oregano
3 Tbs. capers (optional)
¹/₄ cup finely chopped parsley
2 eggs, beaten
¹/₂–1 cup Parmesan and/or Romano cheese,
    freshly and finely grated, to taste
1 Tbs. lemon juice, to taste
¹/₄–¹/₂ cup finely chopped fresh basil
    (optional)

Fry ham or bacon and onions together until
onions are transparent. Add wine, black
pepper, and oregano; simmer until onions
are tender and sauce is fairly thick.

Meanwhile, start pasta in a large kettle with
plenty of salted boiling water with a little oil
in it.

Add squid, garlic, capers, finely chopped
parsley, eggs, basil, to slightly cooled sauce.
Put in large bowl.

Drain pasta in colander. Toss pasta and
sauce together with plenty of cheese and
more black pepper, garlic, and, if it needs it,
a touch of lemon juice.

6 servings

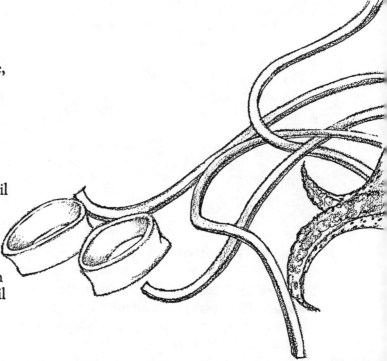

MEE KROB
(THAILAND)

Puffed rice sticks with sweet-tart chicken-ham-squid sauce

1½ lbs. squid, cleaned, bodies in rings,
    tentacles whole or halved
½ onion, diced
1 Tbs. garlic paste, to taste
1 Tbs. grated grapefruit rind and/or grated
    lemon and orange rind, to taste
2 Tbs. yellow bean paste or thick bean paste
    (Chinese), *or* substitute miso
3 Tbs. sugar or brown sugar, to taste (should
    be sweet)
2 Tbs. tamarind water (optional, but lovely);
    or substitute more lemon juice or a
    little vinegar
1 tsp. fish sauce, to taste
2 Tbs. lemon juice, to taste
chili water, to taste
3 Tbs. pickled scallions *or* pickled garlic
    (optional)
½ cup ham slivers *or* pork slivers, to taste
½ cup boneless chicken slivers, to taste
½ bunch of scallions
1 cup bean sprouts
6 fresh chilis, preferably red and small
3 eggs
½ lb. rice stick noodles

Make scallion "brushes." Trim scallions to whites and 2″ of green. Make intersecting cuts in the first inch of each end. Place in ice water and refrigerate.

Make chili "caps." Holding stem, make intersecting cuts from tip almost to stem. Place in ice water and refrigerate.

Fry onions and garlic. Add bean paste, tamarind water, fish sauce, pickled scallions, tomato paste, sugar, chili water. Simmer until mixture is very thick. Fry separately ham (or pork) and chicken. Add to sauce with citrus peel and lemon juice. Let rest.

Meanwhile, beat eggs. Drizzle off your fingers into 350 degree deep fat oil to form lace. Turn after 5 seconds or so until evenly golden brown. Drain on paper towels.

Turn up deep fryer to 400 degrees. Deep-fry handfuls of rice stick noodles at a time, turning when half done to very lightly brown. Drain on paper towels.

For the final assembly, heat sauce, add squid and simmer a few seconds. Toss noodles and sauce together, arrange on platter surrounded by bean sprouts, garnished with drained scallion brushes and chili caps.

4 servings

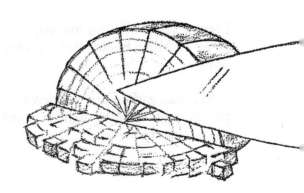

PANCIT
(PHILIPPINES)
Noodles wok'd with calamari, chicken, pork, sausage

1½ lbs. squid, cleaned, bodies in thin rings, tentacles in pieces
½ lb. boneless pork, shoulder or butt
¾ lb. large chicken legs
2 Chinese sausages
2 Tbs. dried shrimp, ground, or ¼ lb. raw shrimp, shelled, deveined, diced
1 tsp. salt
3 Tbs. peanut oil
1 medium onion, very thinly sliced
1 tsp. paprika
1 cup thinly sliced celery
1 lb. fresh Chinese egg noodles, or substitute other fresh pasta, or dried Chinese noodles
2 large garlic cloves, peeled and bruised
2 Tbs. fish sauce, or substitute 2 tsp. anchovy paste crushed in 1½ Tbs. water
2 hard-boiled eggs, shelled and quartered
¼ cup finely chopped green onions
2 lemons, cut into 6 or 8 wedges

Simmer the pork, chicken, sausages, and dried shrimp (if you are using it) together with the salt and water to cover. When meats are tender, strain off stock, reserve. Bone chicken legs, dice chicken, pork, and one of the sausages into ¼" cubes. Slice other sausage for garnish. Sauté onion in 1 Tbs. of the oil until transparent, not brown. Add a tablespoon of water or so as the onion fries to prevent burning, if necessary.

Add paprika, diced pork, sausage, chicken, and the raw shrimp (if you are using it) and continue to stir-fry a minute or so. Add the celery and the calamari, stir a couple of seconds, then remove sauce from heat and keep warm.

Bring reserved cooking liquid to boil. To maximize the flavor of the dish, add as little extra water as necessary to cook noodles, much less than would be used normally. Stir in noodles, stirring constantly until tender to the bite, about a minute for fresh noodles and anywhere from 3 to 9 minutes for dried. Drain noodles, saving stock for another use *or* concentrate down to glaze and add to sauce. Run cold water over noodles to stop cooking.

Fry garlic cloves in skillet in remaining oil until it browns. Discard garlic, add noodles, stir-fry a couple minutes. Stir in fish sauce.

Serve noodles on platter with calamari sauce over them. Garnish with sliced sausage, eggs, green onions, and lemon wedges.

4 servings

PAELLA
(SPAIN)

Saffron rice with calamari, chicken, sausage, and lobster

1¹/₂–2 lbs. live lobster
2 lbs. squid, cleaned, bodies in rings, tentacles whole
¹/₂ lb. chorizo, linguica, or other spicy sausage
1 small chicken, cut into 12 serving pieces
2 tsp. salt
freshly ground pepper, to taste
¹/₂ cup olive oil
1 medium onion, finely diced
1–2 tsp. garlic paste
1 medium bell pepper, red or green, sliced
³/₄ cup tomato puree
3 cups white rice
¹/₄–¹/₂ tsp. saffron threads (The real thing is important to this dish.)
6 cups boiling water
1 6-ounce jar artichoke hearts, preferably marinated
12 lemon wedges from 2 lemons

The meats and seafoods used in this dish are flexible as to amount and kind. Clams or mussels are often used. With a cleaver or large, heavy knife, chop off the tail section of the lobster at the point where it joins the body and twist or cut off the large claws. Remove and discard the gelatinous sac (stomach) in the head and the long intestinal vein. Cut the tail crosswise into inch-thick slices. Quarter the body.
Simmer the sausages in water to cover for 5 minutes. Drain and slice into ¹/₄" rounds.

In a skillet, richly brown the chicken pieces, seasoned with half the salt and the pepper, in half the olive oil over high heat. Remove chicken.

Sauté lobster pieces in remaining oil for a few minutes, then lightly brown the sausage slices. Discard oil. Without cleaning the skillet, add the remaining ¹/₄ cup olive oil, and sauté the onion with the remaining salt over high heat. After a minute or so, add the garlic, pepper slices, and tomato puree. Continue cooking and stirring constantly until mixture thickens heavily.

Preheat oven to 400 degrees about half an hour before you plan to serve the paella. In a 14-inch paella pan, skillet, or casserole at least the equivalent of 14" diameter and 2–2¹/₂" deep (a conventional wok is too deep), combine the sautéed vegetables, the rice, 1–1¹/₂ tsp. more salt, to taste, and the saffron. Pour in the boiling water and bring to a boil, stirring constantly. Arrange chicken, calamari, sausages, artichoke hearts, lobster pieces on top. Put pan on floor of the oven and bake uncovered 25–30 minutes.

Remove paella from oven, cover with a kitchen towel, let stand 5 minutes or so. Serve with lemon wedges.

6–8 servings

RISOTTO CON CALAMARI, SCAMPI, E MUSCOLI

(ITALY)

Venetian saffron rice with squid, shrimp, and mussels

1 lb. squid, cleaned, bodies in 1/4" rings, tentacles whole
3 lbs. mussels, well-scrubbed
3 1/2 cups fish stock or clam juice
1/2 cup mussel juice
salt, to taste
1/2 cup sweet butter (preferably) or salted butter
1/2 cup olive oil (less oil and butter can be used, but the result will not be as meltingly succulent)
2 cups Italian short grain rice
1 medium to large onion, finely diced
1 Tbs. garlic paste
1 cup dry white wine
1 1/2 lbs. raw, shelled, cleaned shrimp cut into 1/2" pieces
1/4–1/2 tsp. saffron threads, crumbled
3/4 cup finely chopped parsley
dash fresh lemon juice (if needed)

Cover squid with fish stock or clam juice. Bring to a boil and simmer until tender, about 30–40 minutes. Add mussels during last 5 minutes of cooking. Remove when shells open. Drain squid, reserving stock. Remove beards from mussels. Add saffron to stock and salt to taste, keeping stock at a simmer.

Melt butter and oil in a heavy 3–4 quart saucepan. As oils reach point of maximum fragrance, stir in rice. Keep stirring rice over high heat to coat with fat but not to brown. Stir in onion, sauté until transparent. Stir in garlic paste, sauté until dry.

Add wine, stir until wine is almost evaporated. Add 3/4 of the simmering stock. Cover, cook as slowly as possible for about 10 minutes. Stir rice. Add more stock if it seems needed. Cover, let cook a while longer. If rice is not yet tender, add more stock and cook until liquid is absorbed.

Add squid, mussels, and shrimp; stir in and let cook no more than a couple of minutes. The shrimp should be just pink. Stir in parsley and a squirt of lemon, if needed.

6–8 servings

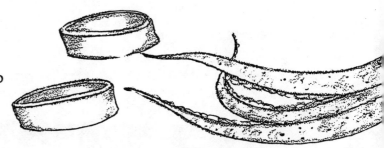

MEE GORENG
(MALAYSIA)
Wok'd pasta with calamari and vegetables

3/4–1 lb. pasta, fresh or dried, rice or wheat
1 1/2 lbs. squid, cleaned and cut in rings, tentacles halved
3 Tbs. oil
1/4 cup ham, slivered
1 cup vegetables, such as green beans, snow peas, zucchini, bok choy, celery, carrots, asparagus, (but not too many different ones), cut into thin strips according to the length of time needed for cooking
1/2 cup bean sprouts
2 Tbs. fresh ginger slivers
1–2 tsp. fresh garlic paste or pieces
2 Tbs. soy sauce, to taste
chili water, to taste
2 Tbs. tomato paste
1 Tbs. brown sugar (optional)
1 Tbs. lemon juice
omelet strips from two egg omelet
cilantro
peanuts
deep-fried onions

Soak rice stick noodles, if used. Otherwise, have large kettle of boiling water, with a little salt and oil. Start wheat noodles to finish 5 minutes after starting next step. Lightly wok ginger and garlic. Add vegetables that take longer to cook—carrots and green beans, for example—add a little water or stock, the tomato paste, sugar, soy sauce, and ham. Wok a while. Add calamari, drained rice stick noodles (if used), and softer vegetables with chili water to taste. Add lemon, balance flavors on the intense side. Drain wheat noodles (if used), toss with wok mixture, adding bean sprouts. Garnish with cilantro, peanuts, and deep-fried onions.

6 servings

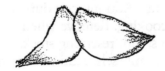

CHARBROILED

KALAMARAKIA GRI-GRI
(GREECE)
Skewered and marinated and broiled squid

1¹/₂ lbs. squid bodies, cut into ¹/₂-inch squares, tightly threaded on small skewers

MARINADE

¹/₂ cup olive oil
¹/₂ cup lemon juice, freshly squeezed
¹/₂ tsp. thyme or oregano
1 tsp. salt
¹/₂ tsp. freshly ground black pepper

Mix marinade to taste, equal parts lemon and olive oil to start. Let skewers marinate at least half an hour. Broil a couple of minutes, preferably over charcoal, basting frequently. Serve, perhaps with French bread and skordalia sauce.

6 servings

SKORDALIA

1 Tbs. walnuts
2 Tbs. cooked potato *or* crustless French bread
2 Tbs. garlic, peeled and chopped, more than seems reasonable
3 Tbs. red wine vinegar and/or fresh lemon juice
¹/₂ tsp. salt
¹/₂ tsp. freshly ground black pepper
¹/₂ cup olive oil (or more)

Blend the first six ingredients in a blender or mortar and pestle, adding water if necessary to obtain a smooth, thin paste.

Balance for tart/salty. Gradually add olive oil with blender running until sauce thickens like mayonnaise.

1 cup

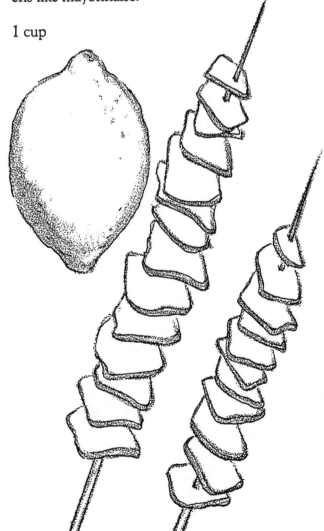

IKA NO MATSUKASA YAKI "PINE CONE SQUID"

(JAPAN)

Scored squid bodies in sake-soy marinade, charbroiled

2 lbs. whole cleaned squid bodies, opened
      flat, scored in crosshatching
1 cup sake
3 Tbs. sugar
1 cup soy sauce
1 cup chicken stock or water
1 Tbs. rice wine vinegar, to taste

Mix last 5 ingredients together. Marinate squid half an hour in all but ½ cup of mixture. Heat this reserved part with 1 Tbs. sugar. When it comes to a boil, stir in 2 Tbs. cornstarch mixed in 1 Tbs. water for use as a glaze.

For maximum dramatic effect, squid may be held open and flat with small bamboo skewers. It will hold more glaze this way. However, it is acceptable for it to curl up tightly.

Place squid on grill, scored side down. Turn after 15 seconds or so, spread with a little of the glaze.

Serve it forth.

6 servings

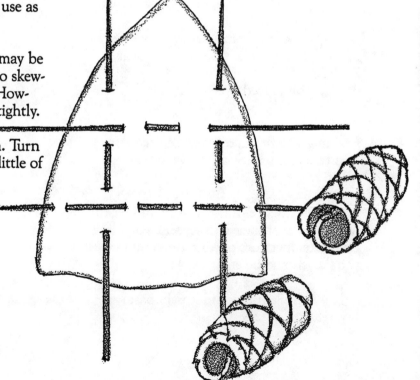

IKA MISOYAKI
(JAPAN)
Grilled calamari with miso sauce

In Japan, one comes across a curious barbeque setup. A charcoal fire or sometimes electric element) is erected vertically. In front of this heat source, large varieties of squid slashed and impaled on stakes sticking out of the ground sputter and sizzle deliciously. The absence of contact with the metal of a hibachi grill means the marinade adheres perfectly and beautifully. I have adapted their procedure, because the recipe is too good to omit.

3 lbs. squid, cleaned, cut and skewered on
      bamboo
1/2 cup miso, preferably yellow or white
3 Tbs. mirin or sake with 1/2 tsp. sugar
2 Tbs. sugar
4 Tbs. sesame seeds, preferably black

Mix miso, mirin, and sugar. Dip skewers into this mixture. Sprinkle with sesame seeds.

Grill over hot fire, turning once and basting with more marinade and seeds. Depending on the temperature of your fire, a minute per side should be enough.

Serve with plain rice and wasabi paste as hot relish.

6 servings

INK DISHES

NOODLES OTHELLO

(USA)

Squid pasta with peas

The colors of this dish are riveting, although the flavor itself is quite mild. The pale blanket of grated Parmesan is Desdemona, so lay it on thick. For less trouble and more flavor, you can alternatively add ink to the sauce at the end of the cooking instead of to the noodles.

NOODLES

3 cups semolina or bread flour (all-purpose will work, but the pasta will lack firmness)
2 eggs
1 Tbs. olive oil
1/2 tsp. salt
8 or so ink sacs (or more if you have them), mashed into 1/4 cup water, membranes strained

Sift flour and salt together. Make a well in the center, pour in the oil, eggs, and ink.

Knead together, adding more flour if necessary. Knead for 10 minutes or so until the dough is satiny. Let rest 10 minutes.

Then, roll quarters of the dough out on a lightly floured board with a rolling pin until it is approximately 1/16 inch thick. Keep moving the dough as you roll it, dusting the top and bottom. Roll the dough up and slice the roll crossways into 1/4 inch noodles. Or, use a pasta machine set for fettuccine. Let the noodles rest.

SAUCE

2 lbs. squid, cleaned and cut into rings, with tentacles
1/4 lb. butter
1/2–1 tsp. garlic paste
1/4–1/2 tsp. anchovy paste (optional but good)
1 lb. fresh tender peas, shelled, or 1/2 lb. slivered snow peas
salt
freshly ground pepper
fresh lemon juice
3/4 cup freshly grated Parmesan cheese

Bring a large pot of salted water to a full boil. Add pasta and a tablespoon of oil. Over high heat, melt the butter with the garlic. Add the peas, sauté briefly. Add the anchovy paste and squid, salt and pepper. Toss together with sauce. Adjust seasoning with lemon, garlic, salt, and pepper.

Serve mounded with Parmesan.

6 servings

ADOBO NEGRO
(PHILIPPINES)
This is a quick black risotto version of Adobo (p. 81)

2 lbs. squid, cleaned, in rings or pieces, tentacles whole

1/2 lb. boneless pork, cut in very thin slices, or bone out the pork yourself and use the bone in the stock

4 Tbs. peanut or olive oil

2 1/2 cups rice, preferably short-grain

1/4–1/2 cup fresh garlic paste

1 tsp. freshly ground black pepper

1/2 cup distilled white vinegar

3 Tbs. soy sauce

4 cups pork or chicken stock

ink sacs, mashed in a little water, membranes strained

tomato wedges and parsley to garnish

Heat oil over high heat. When almost smoking, brown pork briefly, 2–3 minutes. Add dry rice, sauté 2 minutes or so, then add garlic, pepper, and squid. Sauté until squid begins to curl.

Add vinegar, soy sauce, and stock. Bring to a boil, stir in the squid ink, lower the heat to the barest simmer and cover.

After 15 minutes, the stock should be mostly absorbed and the rice tender. If dry, pour more stock or water down side of pan. Do not stir and continue cooking. If too wet, continue cooking a few more minutes. The dish should be moist. Garnish with tomato wedges and parsley.

6 servings

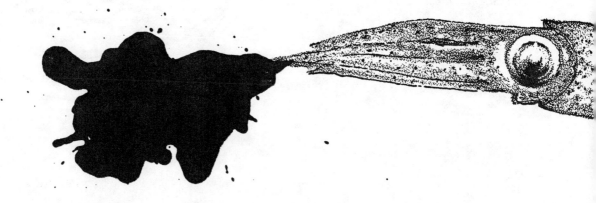

INK TOAST
(FRANCE)
Calamari ink sac spread

The inspiration for this recipe comes from Paula Wolfert, tireless and enthusiastic researcher into squid ink edibles.

4 Tbs. ink sacs, whole (save the punctured ones for another recipe)
1 Tbs. butter
salt, to taste
freshly ground black pepper, to taste
baguette, sliced thin in rounds and toasted

Carefully and gently fry the ink sacs in a small frying pan with the butter until they are set and firm, about 3 minutes over medium-low heat. Place or spread pieces on buttered baguette rounds. Salt and pepper. A squirt of lemon can be nice, but garnish should be kept to a minimum to point up the unique flavors.

4 servings

CALAMARES ALLA ALMENDRAS NEGRAS
(SPAIN)

Calamari sautéed in black almond sauce

The Moorish influence comes through in this dish.

3 lbs. squid, cleaned and chopped
1/4 cup olive oil
1 medium onion, finely diced
1 red bell pepper, sliced
1 green bell pepper, sliced
1/2 lb. mushrooms, sliced
1/2 cup almond butter or food-processed
    toasted almonds
1/2 cup dry white wine
1/2–1 cup stock (chicken, fish or prawn)
salt
freshly ground black pepper
1 Tbs. red wine vinegar, to taste
reserved ink sacs, mashed in water, mem-
    branes strained out

Sauté onion, bell peppers, and mushrooms until clear and soft in olive oil.

Add almond, wine, stock, salt, and pepper. Adjust consistency of sauce until like light cream with additional stock. Simmer for ten minutes. Sauce should be very thick. Add squid and sauté until it waters out and is almost done.

Add ink.

Balance seasoning with vinegar, salt, and pepper.

Serve with French bread.

6 servings

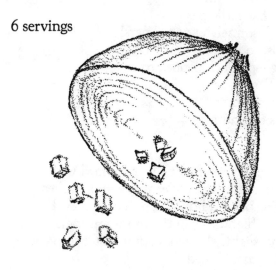

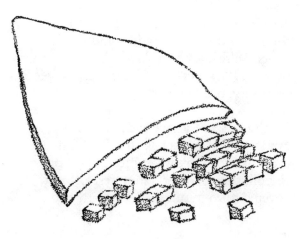

CALAMARES EN SU TINTA
(SPAIN)
Squid braised in its own ink

12 cleaned squid bodies in rings, tentacles
       halved
3 Tbs. olive oil
$1/2$ onion, finely chopped
2 Tbs. garlic paste
3 Tbs. finely chopped parsley
salt, to taste
$1/2$ tsp. black pepper, to taste
2 Tbs. flour
1 cup water
$1/8$ tsp. nutmeg

Carefully reserve ink sacs in bowl with a
little water when cleaning squid. Preheat
olive oil. Add onions, garlic, parsley. Fry
over high heat, until onions are transparent
and slightly brown, adding water to prevent
burning, if needed.

Or fry squid along with onions. In any case,
then turn down heat, add squid if you
haven't already, cover skillet tightly, simmer
over very low heat 20–30 minutes, longer if
necessary, until tender.

Mash ink sacs in sieve with back of spoon.
Add water to extract all ink. Whisk flour
into ink. Pour ink-water into skillet. Bring
to boil, then simmer 5 minutes. Let rest,
covered for 5 minutes. Serve with rice.

4 servings

INDEX

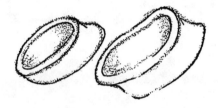